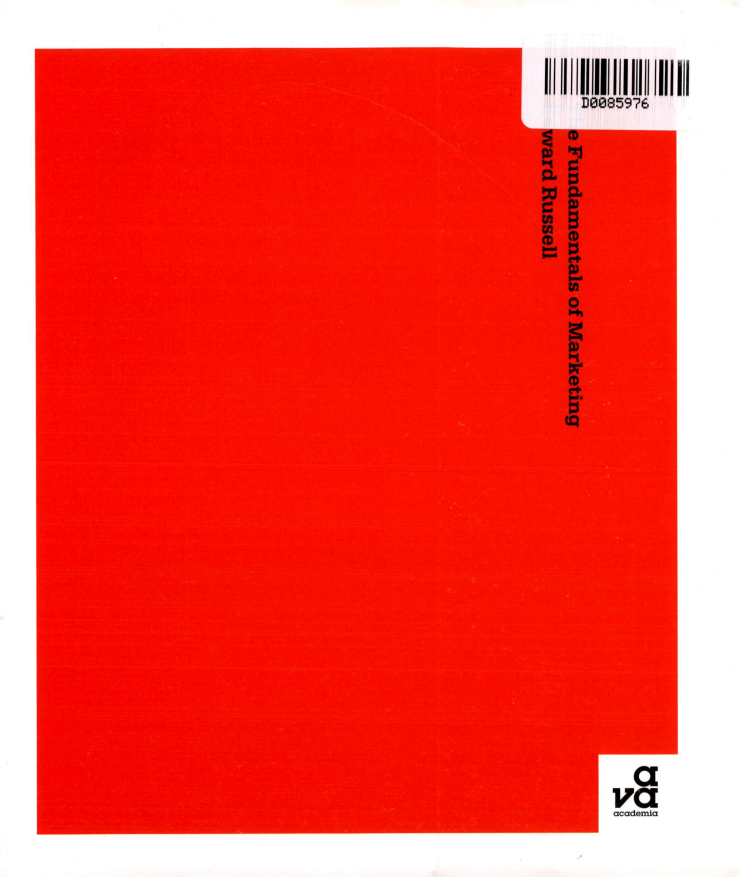

e Fundamentals of Marketing
ward Russell

ava
academia

An AVA Book

Published by AVA Publishing SA
Rue des Fontenailles 16
Case Postale
1000 Lausanne 6
Switzerland
Tel: +41 786 005 109
Email: enquiries@avabooks.ch

Distributed by Thames & Hudson (ex-North America)
181a High Holborn
London WC1V 7QX
United Kingdom
Tel: +44 20 7845 5000
Fax: +44 20 7845 5055
Email: sales@thameshudson.co.uk
www.thamesandhudson.com

Distributed in the USA & Canada by:
Ingram Publisher Services Inc.
1 Ingram Blvd.
La Vergne TN 37086
USA
Tel: +1 866 400 5351
Fax: +1 800 838 1149
Email: customer.service@ingrampublisherservices.com

English Language Support Office
AVA Publishing (UK) Ltd.
Tel: +44 1903 204 455
Email: enquiries@avabooks.ch

ISBN 978-2-940373-72-7

10 9 8 7 6 5 4 3 2 1

Design by Roger Fawcett-Tang

Production by AVA Book Production Pte. Ltd., Singapore
Tel: +65 6334 8173
Fax: +65 6259 9830
Email: production@avabooks.com.sg

Edward Russell

The Fundamentals
of Marketing

Contents

→ Introduction
→→ The business of marketing

Contents

Introduction

The purpose of this book is to teach you the basics of how marketing organisations successfully move from product concept through to the creation of successful brands. We will look at the tools used to develop successful brands including selling theories, consumer behaviour, creation and development of brands, strategic pricing, various methods of distribution, market research, strategic thinking and the promotion of brands through advertising and various other methods.

Every successful marketing person needs four strong characteristics:

- An insatiable curiosity about people and their lives
- Vision to see beyond reality into possibility
- A mastery of every marketing tool at their disposal
- An ability to turn complex business situations into simple communications

Successful marketers are naturally curious people. Marketing requires a stunning amount of research, analysis, comprehension, interpretation, translation, testing hypotheses and openness to new ways of looking at the world. An insatiable curiosity to understand why people do what they do and the ability to move beyond a basic understanding into real insight will help you to be a successful marketer.

Truly great marketers are those who can see beyond the present reality to future possibilities. Consider the visionary products of our generation; the personal computer, MP3 players, the iPhone and so many others. These products only became successful because someone could see their possibilities. 10,000 CD-quality songs in your pocket?

Absurd a decade ago and old news today. Free Internet radio that only plays songs you love? Absurd a decade ago and today called Pandora.com and a variety of other names. Living a 'second life' in contact with complete strangers around the globe? Today millions participate every day because someone saw beyond reality into possibility.

However, vision alone isn't enough. Having mastery of every tool at your disposal will allow you to build a brand that stands the test of time. Brands are created and built primarily through communications. The ability to turn complex business situations into simple communications will help your brand become an icon of the future. We will learn this talent.

Marketing is one of the most powerful forces on Earth. It creates tremendous wealth. It gets candidates elected. It can help build strong and productive societies, but it can equally be one of the most destructive forces on Earth.

This book looks at the best of marketing theory through the practical eyes of a long-time practitioner. Since marketing is a 'learn-by-doing' subject, we will have lots of practice sessions and suggestions. You'll even have the opportunity to put together a marketing plan for a new product called the 'Smart Battery'. Integrate these principles and techniques into your daily life and you are on your way to becoming a successful marketing practitioner.

The goal is simply to give you the basic knowledge and skills you will need to be successful in the marketing industry.

So let's get to work!

Chapter by chapter

1) The business of marketing

We will begin in Chapter 1 with a holistic understanding of the practice of marketing. We will see how professionals develop products, determine pricing, gain distribution and develop marketing communications to build powerful brands.

2) Consumer behaviour and target audiences

What is the centre of truly successful marketing? The consumer. Brands are successful only if someone buys them. It all starts with the wants, needs, dreams and desires of real people just like you. A thorough understanding of consumer behaviour is critical to success in marketing and we'll start with the consumer in Chapter 2.

3) Product and brand development

In Chapter 3, we will look at how a product becomes a brand. Even more importantly, we will look at how some brands inspire passion on behalf of their consumers to the point they become 'evangelists' for the brand. We will look at the role your competition plays in keeping you on your toes and discuss how brands are built and managed.

4) Strategic pricing and value marketing

How do you determine the optimal price for your product? Pricing can be a strategic weapon against your competition or it can run you out of business. What's the difference between price and value? Chapter 4 will look at how prices are determined and how you can maximise your overall profitability through pricing.

5) Distribution channels marketing

Where is the best place to see your brand? Exclusive stores? The Internet? Mass discounters? Where you sell your brand could have just as much impact on your overall success as pricing or advertising. Distribution is yet another marketing tool you'll need to manage in order to maximise the overall impact of your marketing plan. We'll get you started in Chapter 5.

6) Promotion in marketing

When most people think about marketing, they think of marketing communications; advertising, coupons, sampling, and the many tools of the promotion tool chest. Chapter 6 will take a good look at how marketing communications work as well as what we can learn from marketing communications that do not work. We will discuss how marketing communications are developed. We will look at each position in a marketing communications firm; discuss how they create strategies that guide the work and the actual commercials, websites and billboards that we see.

Finally, the most important part of any marketing plan is its effectiveness. In most cases, you have one shot at producing an effective marketing plan. If your plans don't work, the cost could be enormous and maybe even kill your brand. The final part of Chapter 6 discusses how to judge and measure the effectiveness of your marketing plan with an emphasis on predictive measurement.

←← Contents
→ **Introduction / Chapter by chapter**
→→ How to get the most from this book

7

How to get the most from this book

The Fundamentals of Marketing is your introduction to the theory and practice of marketing. You'll learn how products go from an initial concept to become successful brands with qualities and audiences worth far more than the tangible product. Marketing, like most things in life, is a 'learn-by-doing' proposition. You can't learn it all in this or any other book. You learn it by doing it. This book is designed to give you the tools you'll need to begin participating as a practitioner.

Read the book and do the exercises… over and over. You'll soon see yourself thinking like a marketing practitioner thinks and developing simple solutions to complex problems.

Box outs
Key information is featured in box outs for clarity and emphasis.

Quotes
Tips from the masters of marketing who have created some of the most successful brands in the world.

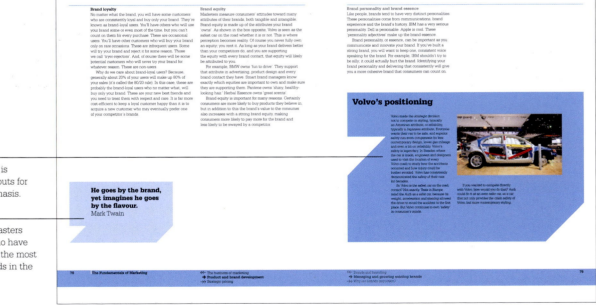

Brand loyalty
No matter what the brand, you will have some customers who are consistently loyal and buy only your brand. They're known as brand-loyal users. You'll have others who will use your brand some or even most of the time, but you can't count on them for every purchase. These are occasional users. You'll have other customers who will buy your brand only on rare occasions. These are infrequent users. Some will try your brand and reject it for some reason. Those we call 'tryer-rejectors'. And, of course there will be some potential customers who will never try your brand for whatever reason. These are non-users.

Why do we care about brand-loyal users? Because, generally about 20% of your users will make up 80% of your sales (it's called the 80/20 rule). In this case, these are probably the brand-loyal users who no matter what, will buy only your brand. These are your new best friends and you need to treat them with respect and care. It is far more cost-efficient to keep a loyal customer happy than it is to acquire a new customer who may eventually prefer one of your competitor's brands.

Brand equity
Marketers measure consumers' attitudes toward many attributes of their brands, both tangible and intangible. Brand equity is made up of the attributes your brand 'owns'. As shown in the box opposite, Volvo is seen as the safest car on the road whether it is or not. This is where perception becomes reality. Of course you never fully own an equity; you rent it. As long as your brand delivers better than your competitors do, and you are supporting the equity with every brand contact, that equity will likely be attributed to you.

For example, BMW owns 'fun to drive'. They support that attribute in advertising, product design and every brand contact they have. Smart brand managers know exactly which equities are important to own and make sure they are supporting them. Pantene owns 'shiny, healthy-looking hair.' Herbal Essence owns 'great scents'.

Brand equity is important for many reasons. Certainly consumers are more likely to buy products they believe in, but in addition to this the brand's value to the consumer also increases with a strong brand equity, making consumers more likely to pay more for the brand and less likely to be swayed by a competitor.

Brand personality and brand essence
Like people, brands tend to have very distinct personalities. These personalities come from communications, brand experience and the brand's history. IBM has a very serious personality. Dell is personable. Apple is cool. These 'personality adjectives' make up the brand essence.

Brand personality, or essence, can be important as you communicate and innovate your brand. If you've built a strong brand, you will want to keep one, consistent voice speaking for the brand. For example, IBM shouldn't try to be silly; it could actually hurt the brand. Identifying your brand personality and delivering that consistently will give you a more cohesive brand that consumers can count on.

Volvo's positioning

Volvo made the strategic decision not to compete on styling, typically an American attribute, or reliability, typically a Japanese attribute. Everyone wants their car to be safe, and superior safety can even compensate for less contemporary design, lower gas mileage and even a bit on reliability. Volvo's safety is legendary. In Sweden where the car is made, engineers and designers used to visit the location of every Volvo crash to study how the accidents occurred and how injury could be further avoided. Volvo has consistently demonstrated the safety of their cars for decades.

So Volvo is the safest car on the road, correct? Not exactly. Tests in Europe rated the Audi as a safer car, because its weight, acceleration and steering allowed the driver to avoid the accident in the first place. But Volvo continues to own 'safety' in consumer's minds.

If you wanted to compete directly with Volvo, how would you do that? Audi could do it at an even safer car, or a car that not only provides the crash safety of Volvo, but more contemporary styling.

> **He goes by the brand, yet imagines he goes by the flavour.**
> Mark Twain

Case studies
Detailed case studies offer insight into the working methods of some of the world's most successful practitioners.

Images
Images and captions illustrate examples of successful campaigns.

Case study: Amazon.com and analytics

Amazon.com knows that I love Celtic music and suggests new artists I might like, allows me to sample their albums and links me to even more artists I might never hear about any other way. Similarly, when I bought Al Gore's *An Inconvenient Truth* DVD, Amazon began suggesting environmentally friendly cleaning products, energy-efficient light bulbs and more. But they offer even more than that…

I encourage my students to buy textbooks from Amazon Why? Because you almost never pay full price and you even get an option to buy used versions from a variety of sellers. This guarantees you get the best product at the best possible price. And that's what Amazon is all about: an online consumer-centric store where customers can find anything they want at the lowest possible prices.

How do they do it?
How does Amazon know me so well? Analytics. Analytics is the new buzzword for tracking consumers' viewing and buying habits, compiling a profile of each customer in order to predict future behaviour. Amazon's computer program tracks everything I do on their site (cyber-observation). That's not unusual, but they've taken it a step further in order to use that information to recommend other products and services they believe I might like as well.

In a world of fewer and fewer true product innovations and less product superiority, marketers are turning to analytics to get to know their consumers better and therefore better serve their needs. For example, let's take a look at Internet radio station Pandora, which creates a radio station based on the user's favourite artists or songs. Pandora's Music Genome Project dissects a song using 400 different attributes to try to match it to songs that have been composed with similar themes, similar instrumentation, similar vocal styles and so on. The station then streams music of a similar genre allowing the listener to hear new music and new artists they are predicted to like. And it works.

If this works so well for music, what else might it work well for? Books? DVDs? Electronics? Food items? Cosmetics? Clothes? Sports equipment? What wouldn't it work well for? Companies such as Procter & Gamble, Netflix, Capital One Credit Cards and thousands more are getting into the business of statistically analysing their consumers in order to better predict their future wants and needs.

Analytics can also increase the value of each sale. For example, I recently heard a Celtic harpist named Aine Minogue on Pandora.com and decided to buy one of her CDs. I was able to click right on the 'Buy CD at Amazon' button and go directly to the CD. The CD was listed at $16.98. In addition, Amazon put together three of her most popular CDs (since they know I have never ordered any of these before) for the low price of $50.94 (note, that is merely $16.96 times three). Below that they tell me that customers who bought Aine Minogue's CD also bought CDs from Enya, Loreena McKennitt and others. That tells me other music I'm likely to want. I can sample every song on the CD and buy it as a CD or an MP3 download. There are three more attempts on the page to introduce me to similar artists and lists of similar music. Amazon has turned the search for a single CD into a musical education on Celtic harpists with many options aimed directly at me.

Moral of the story
The better you know your customer, the better you can serve them and the more loyal they will become. Amazon started business in 1995 and is the largest retailer on the Internet. Why? Because they know their customers better than anyone else. They know what they buy and what they reject largely through their use of consumer analytics. While compiling consumer analytics is nothing new, the ability to use that information to make real-time product recommendations is a relatively new phenomenon and one that every serious marketer has to look at as a way to build their business going forward. We like what we like and don't like what we don't like. If marketers can efficiently compile that knowledge, they can actually make marketing as consumer-focused as it claims to be.

Amazon top 'The American Customer Satisfaction Index'
According to The American Customer Satisfaction Index (ACSI), an independent measure of US consumer opinion, Amazon.com leads the way in online customer satisfaction. ACSI reports scores on a 0–100 scale and in 2001 and 2002 Amazon scored the highest ever customer satisfaction rating (84/100 in 2001 and 88/100 in 2002). Both service and the value proposition offered by Amazon have impressed at a steep rate and it will remain one of the strongest exponents of customer satisfaction in the world.

66   The Fundamentals of Marketing   ← The Business of Marketing   67
→ Consumer behaviour
→→ Product and brand development

Smart plan
Each chapter concludes with a detailed exercise based around the development of a full marketing plan for a new product called a Smart Battery.

Student exercises
Exercises offer the opportunity to put the theory into practice.

Smart plan: Part one

How to build a marketing plan
During the course of this book, you will learn everything you need to know to create a basic marketing plan. Once you have a plan, all you really need to do is execute that plan in order to build a successful business of your own.

Our product for this ongoing section will be a new category of batteries that we'll call a smart battery. The battery lasts 10 times as long as a conventional alkaline battery because it has the ability to turn itself off when not in use.

You see, a normal alkaline battery slowly drains power from the time it is manufactured and placed into the package. Obviously the power is drained more quickly when the battery is in use, but a normal battery can't shut itself off. Our new smart battery contains a microchip that simply shuts the battery down when it's not in use.

Think about how often you actually use many of the batteries in your home. How many hours do you use a flashlight? How many hours is it turned off? The same is true of any battery powered appliance you have. Even the most popular games might be used for an hour a day and turned off the other 23 hours. Imagine the impact of being able to completely stop the power drain during the time the battery is not in use. This is not a hypothetical product, I've seen them. The manufacturer that created the smart battery technology decided not to introduce the product, but you may be able to figure out how to make it a huge success.

The first question must be, 'does the world want a Smart Battery?' Initial research in the US showed over 80% of the battery buying public said they would definitely try it. Now it's up to you to figure out how to build on that.

Smart Battery: Exercise one
The first step is to understand your relationship to disposable batteries. This will involve visiting retailers and speaking to family members and friends. Complete the following:

You as a battery consumer:
→ Make a list of everything you have at home that uses disposable batteries (do not include built-in rechargeable batteries such as the ones used in MP3 players)
→ Do you know when you last changed each battery?
→ Do you know how long you expect new batteries to work in each item you've listed?
→ How many disposable batteries are you using at any given time?

People research:
→ Discuss battery buying and usage habits with at least four people. Seek to understand how much they know about batteries, how much they care about batteries and their general level of satisfaction with the category
→ Ask where they buy batteries, how much they pay and if they can recall any battery advertising

Product research:
→ Visit at least four different retailers that sell disposable batteries
→ List all the types of batteries (such as alkaline or lithium), list the brands of batteries, list battery sizes, list different sizes of packaging (how many batteries are in each pack?)

Pricing research:
→ List all the pricing for the products you find at the different stores. Figure out a price per battery for comparison

Place (distribution) research:
→ Where are the batteries located in the store? Is there more than one location? Why do you think they are where they are?
→ Can you buy batteries online?

Promotion research:
→ Do a thorough search for battery advertising online.

Summarise all you learned in no more than one page.

Chapter questions and exercises

1   How do you define marketing?
2   Why do you believe most of the classic definitions of marketing make no mention of people?
3   Why do you think most companies create products and then try to figure out how to market them to consumers instead of starting with the consumer in the first place?
4   Name five products that you feel have been well marketed. Give reasons for each.
5   Name five products that you feel have been poorly marketed. Give reasons for each.
6   What can we learn from history that might indicate the future of the marketing industry?
7   Name five companies that practise the classic marketing model as demonstrated by Apple.
8   Name five companies that practise the new marketing model as demonstrated by Google.

The business of marketing

Marketing is a powerful force

Marketing is a powerful force that builds strong global brands; it can help raise an army and can be used to demonise political opponents. Every company and government in the world uses elements of marketing on a daily basis and has done so throughout history. In this book we will learn how marketing works and how you can make marketing work for you.

Ask the average person on the street what marketing is and they'll tell you it's about 'selling stuff'. That's fundamentally true, but marketing is not simply the act of sales, but how that sale is made. We are all surrounded by marketing 24/7 and each of us is already a marketer in our own way.

Chapter 1 will help you:

→ **Develop your own definition of marketing.**
→ **Learn how the professionals practise marketing.**
→ **Discuss marketing's role in business.**
→ **Use the history of marketing to predict where this business is going in the future.**

What is marketing?

How do the professionals define marketing? According to the American Marketing Association, 'marketing is an organizational function and a set of processes for creating, communicating and delivering value to customers and for managing customer relationships in ways that benefit the organization and its stakeholders'.

The World Marketing Association defines marketing as 'the core business philosophy that directs the processes of identifying and fulfilling the needs of individuals and organizations through exchanges which create superior value for all parties'.

And finally, the UK's Chartered Institute of Marketing says that 'marketing is the management process for identifying, anticipating and satisfying consumer requirements profitably'.

If we just look at the commonalities of these three definitions, we can see that, in essence, marketing is;

a) discovering and giving consumers what they want and need, and
b) doing this at a profit.

The four or five 'P's' of marketing

Professor Jerome McCarthy of Michigan State University wrote a book in the 1950s entitled *The Four P's of Marketing: Product, Place, Price and Promotion*. This book provided a clear structure to the oldest profession on the planet and became the very definition of marketing.

In order to better understand marketing, as you read this chapter, develop your own definition of the term. For example, I think of marketing as the manipulation of product, price, distribution (place), promotion and people (target audience) to satisfy consumers at a profit. Manipulation is a charged word, especially when we talk about manipulating people. However, manipulation is important because as a marketer, I control each of the tools of marketing and manipulate them to maximise the impact on the market.

As a marketing manager, I manipulate what a product looks like, smells like, and feels like. I manipulate how much should be charged for my product. I manipulate where it should be sold (and not sold) and finally, I manipulate tools in my promotion tool kit in hopes of enticing consumers to buy my product. These are the four 'P's' of marketing as highlighted by McCarthy. To these we have added a fifth 'P': people.

In the factory we make cosmetics; in the drugstore we sell hope.
Charles Revson

People

Marketers have debated for years whether 'people' should be included as the fifth 'P' of marketing. But without people, there is no point to marketing, which is why I include it here.

Practised well, marketing revolves around the wants, needs and desires of people. Sometimes these needs are physical, such as nutritious food and clean water. Sometimes the needs are psychological such as a need to impress. Sometimes the need is sociological, such as the need to fit into a culture. Or the need to stand out. There are an infinite number of reasons for people to do what they do, want what they want and act as they do. Therefore, effective marketing should begin with an insightful understanding of the consumer.

However, few marketers actually begin with consumers.

Why? Because most marketing starts with the invention of some new product that there may or may not be a market for. 'We've invented a better product, now go find someone to buy it' is all too often the sequence of events. Quite simply, this is why 80% plus of all new products in the US fail in their first year.

No matter what we are selling, there will be some people that are more likely than others to want to buy it. For example, as a non-smoker, it would be a waste of time and money to try to get me to buy your brand of cigarettes. However, if I were a confirmed smoker, I might be interested in trying a new brand I'd never tried. Discovering your ideal target market and learning all you can about why they do what they do will help you determine the best way to present your product to maximise interest.

P

> **There is more similarity in the marketing challenge of selling a precious painting by Degas and a frosted mug of root beer than you ever thought possible.**
> A. Alfred Taubman

Product

Your product is anything that can be offered for sale or use to another individual. It includes the quality of the product, the materials chosen, the colour/size/scent/taste, every physical aspect of the product. It also includes the packaging of the product (for example, is the product protected or available for the world to see?), the design and manufacturing of the product and any research and development underway to discover better ways to make the product. The product 'P' covers everything that goes into the development of the tangible or intangible object.

Price

Price not only pays for your cost of goods and profit, it does much more. Price communicates quite a bit about the product and sets quality expectations. It also segments the audience into those who can afford it and those who can only wish they could. And finally, it even conveys how you should consume the product.

Even an established brand can charge too much or too little. For example, the VW Phaeton was a failure because VW had spent decades convincing us 'the people's car' shouldn't be expensive. Similarly, when the Porsche 914 became known as the 'poor-man's Porsche' (due in part to its low entry-level price) the brand was doomed to failure.

Place

Place refers to where and how you sell your product and is also referred to as distribution. To get this 'P' right you have to decide whether to sell your product in an exclusive boutique or in a huge superstore? Will you make it widely available or in a select few stores? These are important strategic decisions that influence how your product is perceived and the price consumers will be willing to pay for it.

For example how special would a Burberry coat be if you could buy it at a discount store? Some products start with very exclusive distribution, establish a reputation for their brand and then expand distribution. Apple did this with their iPod; which started in exclusive Apple stores and online and is now widely available. Consider how your quality expectations change in regard to low-cost airlines such as Ryanair compared to British Airways. Place can set quality expectations.

Promotion

Any way you choose to promote your product is called promotion in marketing. This includes any form of marketing communication such as advertising, public relations, sales promotion, event marketing, as well as any personal one-on-one selling you do.

There is one other 'P' that gets debated on a regular basis and that is 'profit'. All commercial businesses are in business to make a profit. Profits are good. With profits, businesses can pay their employees more, they can expand their business and hire more people, they can start new businesses. Profits are the lifeblood of capitalism.

As we'll see throughout this book, there are thousands of ways to increase profitability. You can sell more, charge more, widen distribution, shrink distribution, cut the material cost of goods while keeping the same pricing, shrink the amount of product you are selling but increase the price or cut the cost of manufacturing by producing the product in the least expensive factory in the world.

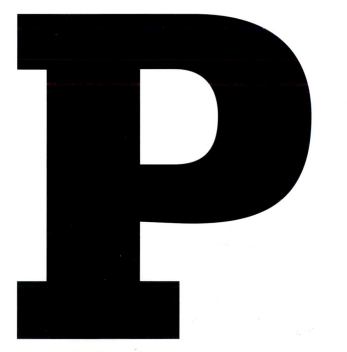

Godiva's 5 P's

Consider the difference between a box of Godiva chocolates and a Mars bar. Both are chocolate, right? If you invite me to dinner at your home and I show up with a box of Godiva chocolates, you are likely to be very happy you invited me. If I show up with a Mars bar, you might not invite me back. What's the difference? Remember, they are both chocolate. Right? Actually no. A Mars bar is an 'everyday' treat, while a box of Godiva chocolates is a selection of 'premium' handmade chocolates. A Mars bar tells the recipient I'm cheap. The box of Godiva tells the recipient I'm very happy to be there, and that they are worth 'the best' I can give. So how do Godiva communicate all this?

People

What kinds of people pay $70/£45 per pound for chocolate? On the surface you might say wealthy people, and you wouldn't be wrong. According to MRI+ (for US only), highly educated women working in business/management positions earning $150,000/£95,000 per year are far more likely to buy Godiva chocolates than anyone else.

However, if you stop there, you would be missing the majority of Godiva customers. Godiva's largest customer group is people buying boxed chocolates as gifts. These may or may not be wealthy people, but clearly they are people trying to impress others with a luxurious gift. The second largest group is 'grazers'. These people can afford a little luxury once in a while. They buy a single piece when they visit the mall. If you go into the Godiva store to buy a single piece of chocolate, you will still be waited on by a highly trained person who can tell you details of every chocolate in the store and will place it in packaging made for a single piece. These people may be looking for a little indulgence, celebrating something good or using the chocolate to get over something bad.

Giving chocolate to others is an intimate form of communication, a sharing of deep, dark secrets.
Milton Zelman, publisher of *Chocolate News*

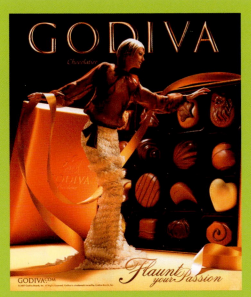

Price

Godiva chocolate can be up to ten times more expensive than its everyday competitors like Mars. So, is it too expensive? No, Godiva uses pricing among other tools to convey quality and exclusivity. If you saw Godiva chocolates priced in line with everyday chocolate bars in your local supermarket it might seem like a bargain at first. However, very soon Godiva chocolate would become commonplace and join the Mars as an everyday product. Pricing therefore signals exclusivity.

Place

Where do you buy Godiva chocolates? The answer? Not just anywhere! You will find Godiva chocolate at exclusive Godiva stores in upscale shopping malls, upscale speciality stores and online <www.godiva. com>. In their upscale stores, the chocolates sit as beautifully lit as Tiffany lights its diamonds. Well trained personnel treat each truffle and filled chocolate much the same way you might treat a fine jewel. You can buy only one and they put it in a small box or bag that isn't all that unlike a jewellery store. And at $3/£2 per piece, you are likely to eat it differently than you might eat a Mars bar. None of this is by accident, it's all part of a larger experience that defines Godiva as a luxury product and keeps you coming back over and over. A Mars bars on the other hand is for sale at corner shops, supermarkets, kiosks and vending machines; the list goes on and on. Consider what the 'place' of a product's distribution says about its 'specialness'.

Promotion

Godiva does advertise… a little. However, as a luxury product, commercial communications need to be very controlled. While Mars could probably advertise as much as they can afford, if Godiva had a large media presence it would be likely to cheapen the appeal of the brand. Godiva promotes primarily through their website (which you should consider 100% advertising), their in-store signage and product presentation and personal one-on-one sales in their company-owned stores.

So, what's the difference between a box of Godiva chocolates and a Mars bar? The answer is basically everything. They may have a few ingredients in common, but little else.

Product

Godiva claim to have invented the concept of premium chocolate from their Belgian headquarters where their chocolates were launched in 1926. Godiva chocolates include every exotic flavour you can imagine. They look perfect, they are fresh, some are handmade, they have a distinctive smell from the cocoa beans used, the texture is stunningly smooth and then there is the taste (I could probably write a chapter on the taste alone). Their chocolate comes wrapped in beautiful gold packaging with a hand-tied bow. Every detail of the chocolate, the packaging and the presentation of this product has been thought through in amazing detail.

Strategic marketing in business

Companies tend to be either product-led, sales-led, finance-led, or marketing-led or consumer led. Each of these types of company acts and reacts differently with varying degrees of success.

Product-led

Historically, most companies were product-led. That is, companies would invent products and then look for a market for the product. Marketing was an afterthought. This product-led philosophy has fuelled many inventive periods in history including the industrial revolution. Even as recently as 1993 with the birth of the Internet, product-led companies developed all around the Internet inventing products that now seem ridiculous. The dot-com bubble burst a few short years later leaving many a product-led company in the dust.

Fashion remains a product-led business. Designers create looks based on what they like, not what you like; and then look for ways to sell it to you. When they are correct in their prediction, the item sells well. When they are incorrect, it doesn't sell. If they have enough successes at creating styles you want, they become major success stories such as Ralph Lauren. If not, they disappear and you never hear of them.

Sales-led

Many companies are sales-led. In sales-led companies, the focus is on selling as much as possible for as long as the product remains viable. Sales-led companies remain viable only as long as their product is viable. Consider the music business. Like the fashion industry, creative individuals create products with the hope that people will hear their creations, like them and be willing to exchange money for them. The business part of the music business concentrates on selling as many CDs, MP3s and live appearances as they can while the musician is a viable product. If the musician doesn't keep up with changing tastes in music, their 'product' has worn out and sales simply go away. That sales-driven company simply moves on to another artist and concentrates on maximising that artist's sales for a period of time. Most sales-led companies tend to fall behind in research and development, get forced into low pricing/profit situations and eventually simply fade away.

Finance-led

Finance-led organisations are run by people more concerned with profitability than anything else. While there is certainly nothing wrong with profitability, finance-led companies tend to become commodity driven businesses and get into the position of squeezing every cent possible out of a business with no differentiation against its competition. Bulk coffee, vegetable oil, gasoline or aspirin products are all made by finance-led companies.

Marketing-led

By the 1960s most major companies became marketing-led organisations. The marketing department directs what products will be researched, developed and produced. They determine pricing strategy (which drives profitability), distribution strategy, the company's outside sales force reports into marketing and they work with specialists from advertising and promotion agencies to develop communications to sell their products. In most major companies around the world, marketing is the centre of everything.

Consumer-led

Consumer-led marketing organisations look for consumer wants and needs and then set out to satisfy those needs at a profit. If you think about most common household goods, you can pretty easily understand how someone articulated a want or need and the marketer set out to supply a product or service to satisfy that need. For example, someone asked for detergents that better protect colours and Procter & Gamble created the detergents to satisfy that need.

Which is best?

Most of the time, marketing-led is best. In a marketing-led corporation, specific people are in charge of maximising the quality of the product, optimising the pricing for consumers and the corporations, maximising the impact of in-store presence and promoting the item in the most impactful and efficient way possible. In a large corporation managing global mega-brands, this can take hundreds of people to deliver a truly optimal marketing plan. However, when done correctly, the impact marketing has on a company is amazing.

However, marketing-led is not always the best model. Marketing-led companies produce what consumers want and need. But what about products consumers can't even conceive of? I seriously doubt that back in 2001 any consumer was asking for a thousand songs on something the size of a coin (let alone 10,000 songs). You can't ask for what you can't conceive of. This product-led invention of the iPod revolutionised how we listen to and buy music. No one asked for it. It wasn't a need. Now we can't imagine living without it.

There is a place for product-led companies, sales-led companies, finance-led companies and certainly marketing-led companies. And please understand, no company is 100% marketing-led or 100% product-led. All are mixtures designed by their creators to maximise their impact in their particular market.

> **You can say the right thing about a product and nobody will listen. You've got to say it in a way that people will feel in their gut. Because if they don't feel it, nothing will happen.**
> William Bernbach

←← What is marketing?
→ **Strategic marketing in business**
→→ A very brief history of marketing

19

A very brief history of marketing

1945–49

To fully understand marketing, you'll need a few basics about its history. With marketing in a constant state of change, an understanding of history will also help you better predict where marketing is headed and how you can help lead these changes.

Marketing has existed since the beginning of human history. Even finding a mate is a form of marketing that includes a product, a price, a place and lots of promotion. As mankind became less self-sufficient and more dependent on others for food, shelter, necessities and entertainment, marketing became a part of everyday life. We didn't call it marketing then… but that's what it was.

Professor E. Jerome McCarthy at Michigan State University became the father of modern marketing with the late 1950s publication of his book *The Four 'P's' of Marketing: Product, Place, Price and Promotion*. With that, marketing was forever 'defined' and marketing was 'born'.

1945–49: After the Second World War
The study and practice of marketing was mostly a post Second World War phenomenon. At the end of 1945 much of Europe was devastated from a war that covered the continent. The economic and military strength of Asia at that time was largely centred in Japan, which was also devastated during the war.

The US, however, was largely untouched by the war. You could even say that the Second World War made the US stronger as a manufacturer and marketer. During the war, the US built state of the art communications systems, distribution systems and modern military factories that were easily retooled to make and sell consumer goods. The returning troops celebrated the end of the war by creating the largest population bubble in the history of America, known as the baby boom. Thus, America had the factories, the infrastructure, the population, the needs and the financial resources to advance consumerism and became the world leader in marketing.

1950s

1960s

1950s: Sell whatever you can make

Five years after the end of the Second World War, Europe and Japan were still recovering and rebuilding from the most devastating war in history. American factories were running at full capacity with mass production and mass distribution of goods. Mass distribution was accompanied by mass advertising for the first time. Factories could sell virtually everything they could make so most concentrated simply on producing as much inventory as possible. Was the quality always the best? No, but that wasn't the priority.

This mass marketing had another effect as well. Because of mass transportation through upgraded rail, air and highway systems, Americans all over the country had access to the same leading brands for the first time ever. Products, taste, even the culture began to homogenise as a result. If you look at Europe since the forming of the European Union you can see some of these same changes occurring.

1960s: Europe makes it better; Asia makes it cheaper

American factories kept focusing purely on quantity of goods. However, American factories were now more than 20 years old. European and Asian factories were brand new and generally far more efficient. America, faced with tough competition for the first time in a generation, was thoroughly unprepared.

Europeans generally produced fewer, higher quality items (think of Mercedes, BMW, Jaguar, and the haute couture fashion houses of Dior, Gucci and others). While Asia, primarily Japan, could produce substantially less expensive goods. The growing electronics business quickly migrated its manufacturing base there and hasn't moved since. As the decade passed, Japanese companies began selling better quality products cheaper than they could be made in the United States.

A mere 15 years after the end of the Second World War, American companies went from having all the advantages, to a highly competitive market where they were caught in the middle – neither manufacturing a high enough quality product nor inexpensive enough product to be successful.

←← Strategic marketing in business
➡ **A very brief history of marketing**
⇢⇢ Where are we headed?

21

1970s

1980s

1970s: Globalise!

What do you do when you produce too much for your country to consume? Simple, look for more customers… globalise!

The search for new customers created yet another trend. With the marketing departments seemingly unable to continue to provide meteoric growth, the nice people in the finance department began to take over as the only group that could continue to grow stock prices; largely by cutting costs. Advertising and brand strength gave way to price promotions in the belief that consumers would buy more if the prices weren't as high. Basically, it didn't work. There are just so many refrigerators and cameras we need, no matter what the price. So, while the sales and marketing departments are opening new markets for American goods around the world, many of the companies are having price wars in the US. With the price wars only decreasing profits more and more, it was time for some new thinking.

1980s: The era of the low cost producer

Looking for increased profitability given that the Marketing division had maximised the number of consumers they could reach, the finance department of major manufacturers began to take more and more control. This time they were able to cut tremendous costs out of the manufacturing of goods, sometimes by cutting inefficiencies out of the process and sometimes by actually cutting quality. Most consumer goods were 're-engineered' to get the best product at the lowest possible cost.

Small changes in product formulations followed one after another, often semi-annually. Every time someone in research and development figured out a way to make the product cheaper, that product would be tested against the product currently on the market. If consumers couldn't see the difference, the product formulation would be changed. The quality of many products declined. One possible reason no one noticed was that reformulations were only tested against the current (often already reformulated) product and not against the 'best' product the manufacturer could make.

Would you be more careful if it was you that got pregnant?
Anyone married or single can get advice on contraception from the Family Planning Association. Margaret Pyke House, 27-35 Mortimer Street, London W1 N 8BQ. Tel. 01-636 9135.

1980s

A prime example of this is Kraft Singles, which began as pasteurised processed cheese slices. As Kraft discovered they could remove cheese from the product and replace it with much cheaper whey, oil, and eventually powdered calcium, the label description changed from 'pasteurised processed cheese' to 'pasteurised processed cheese food' to its current legal definition of 'pasteurised prepared cheese product'. According to the Food and Drug Administration (FDA), they can't even legally label it 'food' in the product descriptor any longer. Did anyone notice? Apparently not. 'Singles' remains one of Kraft's largest brands.

Is there anything wrong with making products more cheaply in order to improve profitability? In a global capitalist economy, the answer is a resounding 'no'. If a manufacturer creates a sub-standard product, another will simply come along with a better product. Remember, nothing happens in a vacuum. When coffee became nothing more than a commodity product with 2–3 brands in a constant price war, along came Starbucks to redefine what a great cup of coffee could be. The same was true in beer. Beer in the US became nearly a commodity business run primarily with price promotions. That gave birth to an entirely new industry of micro-brews and premium imports that have had a dramatic impact on sales.

1990s

1990s: The power is shifting

There are three main players in getting products into your hands: 1) the manufacturer that makes the product 2) the distribution channel (store) that sells the product and 3) you, the consumer. Since the beginning of mass production, the manufacturer had ruled the marketing game. Manufacturers created, produced and sold whatever products they believed consumers would buy. Sometimes they were right and sometimes they were wrong. Stores were simply the 'middle-men' for the most part doing what manufacturers told them they should do.

All that changed with the birth of the Universal Pricing Code (UPC) and scanner, which gave stores instant detailed sales data. The balance of power was thus changed forever. Manufacturers had always known how many items they made and sold to stores. They didn't know how many items consumers actually bought from the store. Stores had a vague idea, but generally relied on once a year inventory checks to measure a year's worth of sales. That's not exactly actionable intelligence.

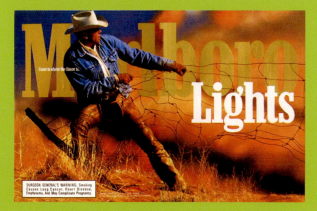

← Strategic marketing in business
→ **A very brief history of marketing**
→→ Where are we headed?

23

1990s

The new data from the scanners gave the stores tremendous power, and they began telling manufacturers what to produce and at what price. They readjusted their store shelves to match the popularity of different brands; kicking out the slow sellers and giving more space to the dominant brands. In general this was a great benefit to large manufacturers and large stores. They could customise each store to match the preferences of their customers. Smaller brands, or slower-moving brands were cast aside and literally thousands disappeared from distribution and most simply died.

When stores took over as the knowledge brokers in marketing, they began to reward their regular customers with frequent shopper programmes. The practice of 'customer management' and 'customer relationship marketing' (CRM) was born. CRM now holds a major position in most major marketing companies. These people are responsible for building long-term relationships between brands and their customers.

2000s

2000s: The consumer in the driver's seat
We've covered 50 years of marketing history with almost nothing said about the consumer. While marketers love to talk about their consumer focus, most really aren't very good at actually focusing their efforts on consumers. The Internet is forcing this change.

Consider how people have shopped for books over the years. In the 1960s most people would shop in their local bookshop where they could browse whatever happened to be in stock and usually purchase their chosen book at the manufacturer's suggested retail price. Next came the mega-bookstores such as Barnes & Noble and Borders where you could view an even larger selection, often at discounted prices. With the Internet, you have virtually every book in the world at your fingertips with sellers such as Amazon.com (plus e-books, published only on the Internet).

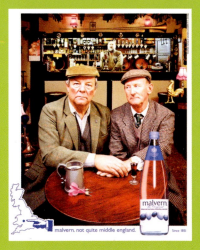

2000s

They are open around the globe 24 hours a day, seven days a week and always sell at a discount. As a consumer, you have moved from whatever your bookstore happened to offer at whatever price they wanted, to greater selection and greater price competition.

Today, the Internet has revolutionised how many businesses operate. No longer do you have to shop for cars by travelling dealer-to-dealer and reading every advertisement. And, no longer do you have to hope you'll get a fair price; the Internet will provide you with multiple offers on everything from books to cars to mortgages and basically anything else you want. Hate grocery shopping? Log onto almost any major supermarket, make your selections and tell the store when you want your groceries delivered.

If information equals power, we have never had more power. The consumer is in charge and manufacturers and stores now truly work for us.

Authentic marketing is not the art of selling what you make but knowing what to make. It is the art of identifying and understanding customer needs and creating solutions that deliver satisfaction to the customers, profits to the producers and benefits for the stakeholders.
Philip Kotler

← Strategic marketing in business
➔ **A very brief history of marketing**
⟫ Where are we headed?

25

Where are we headed?

So, we've seen how marketing has developed over the last few decades, but to be successful in marketing you need to see where we are going. Shopping is a major form of entertainment in many countries around the world and probably always will be. Greater availability of information, opinions and price competition will continue to give consumers more and more power.

Let's take a look at the near-term future to see how we can position ourselves for it.

Demographic trends

As more and more baby boomers retire, we see very different spending habits emerging from the retired. Since the over-55 demographic controls over 70% of the discretionary income in America, we see more and more products aimed at helping this group remain active consumers in today's marketplace.

Income levels continue to polarize. The top 20% of US households currently collect 50% of the total US income. Compare that to the bottom 60% that collects only 27% of US income. Currently 40 million people live below the poverty line, a number that has grown by 17% since the year 2000. With a shrinking middle class, the rich are getting richer and the poor are becoming poorer.

In the US, economic and political power is increasing for women. There are 23% more women than men enrolled in higher education today. Women earn 60% of bachelor's and master's degrees in US colleges. Auto manufacturers are finally recognising that women now buy half of all cars and they are designing cars accordingly.

Retailing has grown to be the #1 entertainment industry. Forget movies, television, books and even the Internet. Shopping has been the #1 entertainment activity for quite a long time. Expect this to grow along with a rash of new retail brands hitting the market, potentially driving some of the old retailers out of business.

Technological changes

Shopping is becoming easier and easier. Soon you will be able to point your phone at a billboard or your TV and have the product being advertised delivered to your home (if you live in parts of Europe and Asia, you can already do this).

Soon, just one screen will give you whatever you want, when and where you want it. Of course there will still be televisions, personal computers and mobile phones but expect whatever you want to be available on the screen of your choice.

What will happen to brands?

Brands are here to stay. Some will grow stronger, some will disappear. Fewer old-world brands will thrive and an influx of new brands will appear. Most of today's hot brands will be replaced within the next decade (or sooner) with brands that don't even exist today, or brands that make a comeback.

With entire industries outsourced in the beginning of the millennium, we can expect even more streamlining of current businesses while an undercurrent of new businesses and new brands rises from smaller, more entrepreneurial companies.

Extinct brand shampoos

What do Breck shampoo, Prell shampoo, Vidal Sassoon shampoo and Pert Plus shampoo have in common? The answer is that at one time they were among the largest shampoo brands in the US and today you practically can't find them on the shelf.

New Beauty Miracle for Younger-Looking Hair!

NEW Prell leaves hair 'Radiantly Alive'

. . . actually **more radiant** than cream or soap shampoos!

Created by Procter & Gamble

Here's proof . . . that marvelous New Prell leaves hair "radiantly alive"! In radiance "comparison tests," New Prell *won over all leading cream and soap shampoos!* Why, the first time you try New Prell, there'll be a difference—no matter what cream or soap shampoo you may have been using. Your hair will shine with glorious radiance . . . will look so "radiantly alive," and will be softer, *younger* looking, more glamorous Not a cream, not a liquid—Prell is *different*. It's the *unique* shampoo in a tube that's such a joy to use—no slip, no break, no spill. Get a tube of New Prell today—you'll *love* it!

⇇ A very brief history of marketing
➡ **Where are we headed?**
⇉ Classic marketers versus the new marketing model

27

Classic marketers versus the new marketing model

Over the past decade a host of new companies have created a new marketing model that relies more on product superiority and accessibility than on promotion. Throughout this book, we'll be looking at both 'classic marketers' and this 'new marketing model'.

Apple Computer:
The classic marketers

Anytime anyone draws up a list of 'cool brands', Apple always pops up on the list. Steve Jobs and Steve Wozniak formed Apple in 1976 after building a computer in Jobs' parent's garage. They named the computer Apple and with the help of a third 'money-partner' set out to produce a simple personal computer. It certainly wasn't the first computer on the market, but it was an attempt to make the computer intuitive enough so that anyone could use it. By 1978, the pair simplified the computer even more with the introduction of the Apple II, which required no software loading; just take it out of the box, plug it in and start using it.

Here's the part that's a big secret; Apple was the global market leader in 1978 selling 100,000 of the Apple II computers. Apple and the two Steves celebrated with a very successful IPO (Initial Public Offering) of its stock.

Steep competition and the rocky road
to world domination

By 1981 the computer world was turned upside down when IBM entered the personal computer market with a computer other competitors could copy and introduce. Within two years, although year-on-year revenue for Apple continued to increase, Apple's global market share fell from 16% to 6%. Apple brought in John Skulley from Pepsi-Cola, hoping that his classic marketing expertise could help the company. The 1984 introduction of the Macintosh along with the famous '1984' TV commercial (played only once on the Super Bowl) was supposed to help capture a greater share of market. Unfortunately, the IBM-type PCs had far more software possibilities, were less expensive than the Macintosh and continued to dominate the global market. By the end of 1984, Apple experienced its first revenue decline and Steve Jobs left the company.

Skulley concentrated the company's resources on capturing the education market (where Apple eventually achieved a 60% share of the market) and began to move more into the corporate world. Skulley introduced classic marketing to Apple. By 'classic' we mean:
1) Develop a new product.
2) Introduce it behind heavy spending in advertising.
3) Work on upgrading and improving the product with upgrades for as long as the market will allow.

Skulley's Pepsi background trained him in the kind of classic marketing that was a hallmark of the cola-wars between Pepsi and Coca-Cola.

←← Where are we headed?
→ **Classic marketers versus the new marketing model**
→→ Case study: The five 'P's' in action

29

Currently, Apple is a shining company, the inventor of the iPod, iPhone, iTouch and a full line of computers at every price point. However, the history is a roller coaster of five Chief Executive Officers in 11 years (including Steve Jobs twice) and a market share that dipped as low as 2%. With Jobs' return in 1997 came new computers, the iPod, the iPhone, new operating systems, the integration of Intel chips allowing Macs to run Windows software, iTunes (Apple's first retail website selling directly to the public) and finally the first Apple store, which opened in 2001. From 1998 to 2007, net sales grew from $6 billion to $24 billion and the year end market value of outstanding stock grew from $5.5 billion to $173.4 billion.

Apple has been an aggressive media spender with approximately 4% of sales, or $500 million going toward media support for the various Apple brands. According to Apple, by the end of September, 2007, computer sales made up about 42% of sales, iPods were 35% of sales, iTunes and related iPod accessories made up 10% of sales and the remaining 13% came from software and hardware.

Keep it fresh

In many ways, Apple is a 'classic' marketer: they create an excellent product, price it right, distribute it well and advertise and promote it vigorously. The difference between Apple and so many other marketers is that Apple has updated everything they do. Their product design defines the state of the art in all their categories. Their pricing is smart and covers nearly every market while supporting a very upscale image. Their distribution goes through state of the art retail stores that created the concept of destination shopping and in many cities are as much a tourist attraction as a retail outlet, and finally, their advertising is big, bold and ubiquitous. Even their recent Mac vs. PC television campaign puts a new spin on the oldest advertising format in the world; the side-by-side comparison.

Google: The new marketing model

Don't you just love that Google advertising campaign with the guy and the girl looking for something and Google saves the day? Oh, you haven't seen it? Neither has anyone. Google does not advertise. That's correct, Google grew from zero to over $20 billion per year in revenue in roughly ten years with no advertising.

Chances are you found out about Google the same way I did; someone told you it was the best search engine in the world and so you gave it a whirl. How did Google do this? And what can we all learn about marketing from Google?

Give the people what they want

Early search engines for sites such as Yahoo relied on a directory listing method. The search engine culled through a list and gave all apparently relevant listings. But within about five years, the web outgrew the ability to search this way. AltaVista created the first search relying on algorithms to more accurately search the thousands upon thousands of sites. The system was better and adopted at first by market leader Yahoo.com for a few years.

Then two graduate students at Stanford University, Sergey Brin and Larry Page, created a page-ranking algorithm that allowed both faster and more accurate searching. With an index of over a billion web pages, Google was the best search engine available. The two licensed this search technology to Yahoo until they began to see that the value went well beyond licensing fees. In 1999, Brin and Page launched Google.com with the help of several venture capital firms.

Keep it simple

We've just looked at marketing as being the manipulation of people, product, price, place and promotion. But what about Google? The target audience is anyone with a computer and Internet connection. The product is superior, but only experientially measurable. The price is free to users, the place is on the Internet anywhere in the world you can log on and the promotion is 100% word of mouth from happy users. That's about as different from the Apple marketing model as you can get, and yet both companies are phenomenally successful.

While Google was profitable licensing its product to third parties such as Yahoo, it wasn't until the launch of Google.com and its paid listing advertising that the real money started flowing. Just like the use of algorithms in the first place, Google didn't invent the paid listing, but did create a way to rank the listings that allowed them to charge more for their service. Brin and Page believed people trying to search the web shouldn't be bogged down with all the extraneous stuff typically found on websites such as Yahoo, so they kept their page clean and free of distractions. Consumers would go there to search and depending on their search, potentially put some more money into Google's pockets by clicking through to one of Google's advertisers.

Within four years, Google managed 75% of all searches in the entire world through its own website and those websites licensing Google technology (such as Yahoo and AOL). Additionally, they launched Froogle (a search engine focused on finding the lowest prices on the web), maps, g-mail, Google Earth and much more.

Google™

← Where are we headed?
→ Classic marketers versus the new marketing model
→ Case studyThe five 'P's' in action

31

Case study: The five 'P's' in action

Let's take a look at some of the most successful marketers in history and see how they became the prominent and powerful marketers they are today. As you'll see, there are plenty of different ways to the top in marketing. We'll also look at some of history's less successful campaigns to see how things could have been done differently.

Intelligence and stupidity on the Internet: People
When the Internet first exploded with e-commerce sites no one really knew how to use it well. Opportunities seemed unlimited and there was investment money flowing freely to anyone with a good idea for this new medium.

After about five years of robust growth, the dot-com bubble burst and suddenly everyone could see much more clearly. An icon of the senseless investment of the 1990s was Pets.com (note the URL is currently owned by another company). The brand tried selling pet food and accessories over the Internet. It launched in 1998 and went out of business in November 2000 when they figured out people weren't willing to buy pet food online, wait for a week until it arrived and pay for the shipping. In hindsight, it seems even more ridiculous that anyone ever thought it would work.

Make it useful!
In Denmark, the Pampers brand managers were frustrated that they had created a beautiful website that almost no one was visiting. Why wouldn't every parent want to log onto Pampers.com and... actually now that I think about it, these people make a convenience product for removing baby's excrement. Who would want to go to a website to learn more about that? I love that Pampers work so well, but I hate everything else about the process.

Apparently the vast majority of Danes agreed with my feelings. But what about Baby.com? Would mothers and fathers log onto Baby.com to learn more about how to take the very best care of their babies? Absolutely they would and they did. Suddenly marketers were starting to realise that consumers loved the Internet for answering questions, researching and learning, but they weren't about to log on just to view adverts. Again, in hindsight that seems so obvious. At the time, not many people knew how to participate in the Internet.

We've come a very long way in a very short time in learning how to effectively use the Internet for brand messages. Take a look at your favourite car company. You can choose a car, build the exact car of your dreams right before your eyes, take a virtual test drive, get competing prices for your dream car and even buy it online. Is that content? Sure, but it's also one of the most amazing in-depth ads you've ever seen. It's all about understanding people's needs and desires.

Procter & Gamble and Unilever: Product

Procter & Gamble (P&G) and Unilever are two of the most powerful and admired global marketers on the planet.

P&G started as a soap and candle company in middle-America (Cincinnati, Ohio) in 1837. Today, P&G's global sales top $84 billion annually with more than 20 brands selling over $1 billion each. Over time the company expanded well beyond detergents and is now a global powerhouse in beauty care, health care and home care. The company has long been admired for its marketing acumen and its training programme is generally considered the best in the world.

Unilever has long been P&G's direct competitor. Started in London in 1890, then called 'Lever Brothers', they started as a soap company in Victorian England. Over the years they expanded throughout Europe and set up a second headquarters for Unilever NV in Amsterdam, Holland. Today Unilever owns more than 400 brands around the world with sales of 40 billion Euros ($29 billion USD).

Superior products
Both companies focus on product superiority in much of their development and marketing efforts.

The global expansion of P&G and Unilever has many parallels. Both began as soap companies and expanded into many categories including food, health care and beauty care. Globally, they practically raced to be the first to sell their range of products in every country. Even today, whichever of the two companies reached a market first generally continues to dominate the categories they have in common even today. For example, India is still a Unilever country, China is still a P&G country.

In the mid-1990s both companies began shedding or shutting down small or unprofitable businesses or brands they felt had maximised their potential. At P&G, iconic brands such as Duncan Hines, Jif peanut butter, Folgers Coffee and Pert Plus shampoo were all sold off. Unilever sold or eliminated 66% of its brands globally (sometimes you get stronger by getting smaller!).

Walk through any food or discount store anywhere in the world and you are likely to see hundreds of brands from P&G and Unilever. In a recent issue of the American product testing magazine, *Consumer Reports*, they ranked the performance of various automatic dish washing products. P&G's Cascade, in its various forms, was ranked numbers one, two, three, four and five. It's all about having superior products.

←← Classic marketers versus the new marketing model
→ **Case study: The five 'P's in action**
→→ Smart plan: Part one

33

Wal-Mart: Price

Sam Walton went to work for the JC Penney company for $75 per month after graduating from college. After bouncing around the Midwest from retail job to retail job, he bought a small store in Bentonville, Arkansas, and opened Walton's 5 & 10. By the end of his life in 1992, Wal-Mart would be the world's largest retailer.

Single-minded focus on low prices

How did a simple man with vision go from being a low-level retail employee to one of the wealthiest and most successful men in the world? By keeping a very single-minded focus on offering the lowest prices in every category he sold. The result? Approximately 80% of disposable diapers sold in the US go through Wal-Mart. About 60% of shampoo and conditioners are sold through Wal-Mart. Quite simply, Walton kept prices low and customers rewarded him with their loyalty.

But how could Wal-Mart sell for less than their competitors at K-Mart and Target stores? Location. While other stores were locating in the centre of large cities, Sam Walton built his stores out in the country between two small towns. The land was cheaper and his Wal-Mart stores could draw customers from both small towns. The result? Walton had as many or more potential customers and did so at a much lower cost than his competitors. Those savings were passed along to customers in the form of some of the lowest prices offered anywhere. The result of this? Very few stores could successfully compete with Walton's prices and all the family retailers that make up a small town began closing up as they lost their customers to Wal-Mart.

As scanners and UPC codes expanded, suddenly Wal-Mart controlled a tremendous amount of information about the sales of every brand they handled. They knew better than anyone exactly what was selling minute by minute, category by category. Soon, they were telling manufacturers how much they were willing to pay for products. Manufacturers were then left trying to figure out how they could make the goods for the price Wal-Mart were willing to pay. This spurred the growth of off-shore manufacturing closing thousands of factories in the US and Europe in favour of shipping manufacturing to less expensive manufacturing countries such as India and China.

Wal-Mart is a controversial company to say the least. It's also stunningly successful. As Sam Walton famously said to his critics, if he wouldn't have done this, someone else would have. For Wal-Mart it's all about low prices.

Tampax: Place

For many of you, tampons are just a normal product. However, this product may be one of the most controversial in the world. Tampon sales are actually banned in some countries as immoral and while legal in Latin America, it's still a cultural taboo.

So, how do you sell a legal product that is considered 'sinful' to use? One of the smartest marketing strategies I've ever heard was the strategy employed by the head of marketing for Tampax in Spain. This person knew selling tampons in Spain was a difficult task. Step one: normalisation. If people, men and women, simply saw Tampax day after day eventually the product would seem normal and a perfectly valid option for women in Spain. A goal was therefore set that you couldn't walk for more than two minutes in any direction in Madrid without seeing an outdoor billboard, a store window display, a logo on a shop door or an ad on the side of a city bus promoting Tampax.

Sure enough, simply by seeing the package everywhere, much of the mystery and fear that surrounded the brand simply disappeared. For Tampax it's all about place!

The automotive industry: Promotion

On average in the US it takes roughly $2,500 advertising to sell each car. Obviously some cars take more, some take less. And while that number should seem high to you, you should also remember that the car manufacturers aren't paying that, it's passed along to the customer in the increased cost of the car. Why is it so much? In part it's because the US auto business is overly branded. Consider European companies such as BMW and Mercedes. Each company makes at least a dozen different models, but they are all known as and sold as BMWs or Mercedes. BMW simply adds a number to their brand name (3 series, 5 series, and 7 series) and Mercedes adds a letter (C Class, S Class and E Class). Advertising for one BMW therefore has impact across the entire brand.

Now contrast that with the American and Japanese car companies. General Motors has eight brands broken down into nearly 100 sub-brands. Advertising for a Chevrolet Corvette has no impact on a Chevrolet Impala and vice versa. Toyota and Honda are no better. It's not a Toyota, it's a Corolla or a Prius or a Camry or a Highlander And then that's not enough. It's a Toyota, Highlander, Limited, Hybrid.

It takes a lot of advertising to sell a car
It's no surprise that advertising for automobiles is one of the highest spending categories in the world. The auto companies have so completely over-branded their cars, it takes a lot of money just to explain that to the public. At one time during the 1970s General Motors started sub-branding their interiors as 'Body by Fisher'. So what? It's not like you could get the interior of your GM car or truck made by someone else. For the car companies, and a lot of other product categories, it's all about promotion.

←← Classic marketers versus the new marketing model
→ **Case study: The five 'P's in action**
→→ Smart plan: Part one

35

Smart plan: Part one

How to build a marketing plan

During the course of this book, you will learn everything you need to know to create a basic marketing plan. Once you have a plan, all you really need to do is execute that plan in order to build a successful business of your own.

Our product for this ongoing section will be a new category of batteries that we'll call a smart battery. The battery lasts 10 times as long as a conventional alkaline battery because it has the ability to turn itself off when not in use.

You see, a normal alkaline battery slowly drains power from the time it is manufactured and placed into the package. Obviously the power is drained more quickly when the battery is in use, but a normal battery can't shut itself off. Our new smart battery contains a microchip that simply shuts the battery down when it's not in use.

Think about how often you actually use many of the batteries in your home. How many hours do you use a flashlight? How many hours is it turned off? The same is true of any battery powered appliance you have. Even the most popular games might be used for an hour a day and turned off the other 23 hours. Imagine the impact of being able to completely stop the power drain during the time the battery is not in use. This is not a hypothetical product; I've seen them. The manufacturer that created the smart battery technology decided not to introduce the product, but you may be able to figure out how to make it a huge success.

The first question must be, 'does the world want a Smart Battery?' Initial research in the US showed over 80% of the battery buying public said they would definitely try it. Now it's up to you to figure out how to build on that.

Smart Battery: Exercise one

The first step is to understand your relationship to disposable batteries as well as the basics of marketing for the category. This will involve visiting retailers and speaking to family members and friends. Complete the following:

You as a battery consumer:

→ Make a list of everything you have at home that uses disposable batteries (do not include built-in rechargeable batteries such as the ones used in MP3 players).
→ Do you know when you last changed each battery?
→ Do you know how long you expect new batteries to work in each item you've listed?
→ How many disposable batteries are you using at any given time?

→ **People research:**
→ Discuss battery buying and usage habits with at least four people. Seek to understand how much they know about batteries, how much they care about batteries and their general level of satisfaction with the category.
→ Ask where they buy batteries, how much they pay and if they can recall any battery advertising.

→ **Product research:**
→ Visit at least four different retailers that sell disposable batteries.
→ List all the types of batteries (such as alkaline or lithium), list the brands of batteries, list battery sizes, list different sizes of packaging (how many batteries are in each pack?)

→ **Pricing research:**
→ List all the pricing for the products you find at the different stores. Figure out a price per battery for comparison.

→ **Place (distribution) research:**
→ Where are the batteries located in the store? Is there more than one location? Why do you think they are where they are?
→ Can you buy batteries online?

→ **Promotion research:**
→ Do a thorough search for battery advertising online.

→ **Summarise all you learned in no more than one page.**

Chapter questions and exercises

1 **How do you define marketing?**
2 **Why do you believe most of the classic definitions of marketing make no mention of people?**
3 **Why do you think most companies create products and then try to figure out how to market them to consumers instead of starting with the consumer in the first place?**
4 **Name five products that you feel have been well marketed. Give reasons for each.**
5 **Name five products that you feel have been poorly marketed. Give reasons for each.**
6 **What can we learn from history that might indicate the future of the marketing industry?**
7 **Name five companies that practise the classic marketing model as demonstrated by Apple.**
8 **Name five companies that practise the new marketing model as demonstrated by Google.**

Consumer behaviour

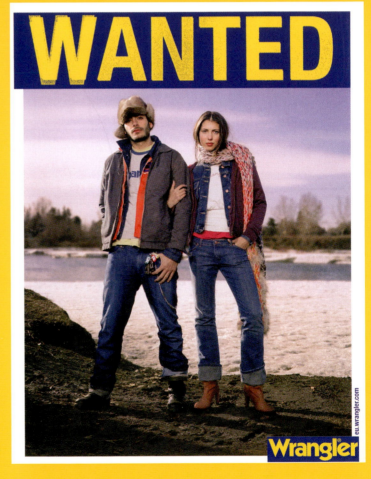

Wrangler jean culture

An advertising agency working with Wrangler jeans hired a team of anthropologists to study 'Wrangler culture'. The anthropologists studied Wrangler wearers and found they wore Wrangler to work all day. Wrangler was considered a 'real-man jean'. However, when these same men came home, they put on a pair of Levi's to go out to the bar at night. They would *never* wear Wrangler to the bar and *never* wear Levi's to work. While Wrangler was macho, it said blue-collar labourer and that wasn't a message they wanted to send while trying to attract women. And while Levi's looked and fitted well, it was a fashion item, not something 'real men' would work in. Do I need to remind you that both are nearly identical pairs of jeans? The cut and cloth may be the same, but the culture each has created is quite different.

Since marketing can only exist in a consumer-driven world, it makes sense to start the study of marketing with the so-called fifth 'P' – People. Successful marketers must have a deep and thorough understanding of consumers' attitudes, behaviour, and most importantly, why they do what they do.

Chapter 2 will help you:

➜ **Understand consumer behaviour.**
➜ **Understand and begin practising market research.**
➜ **Understand what makes people different from each other and how that affects their behaviour.**
➜ **Understand why so many brands fail.**

What is consumer behaviour?

Consumer behaviour is the study of why people do what they do. The better we can understand the rational, emotional and often subconscious reasons for consumers' actions, the better we will be at creating effective marketing campaigns.

Does good marketing always make people do what we want them to do? No. But it can present our brand's story in the best possible light. In order to do this it is important to understand what consumers want, how they make decisions, why they choose the brands they do and how and where we should talk to them.

Spend an hour in a grocery store watching other people shop. You will see a variety of different kinds of shopper. Some are focused people on a mission trying to fulfil a specific list of goods. You will see others slowly comparing products side by side, deciding what they want as they go along. Others are focused on getting the best deals through sales, coupons and volume deals. And still others wander the aisles looking for inspiration as to what they should prepare for the week.

Methods for studying consumer behaviour

Studying consumer behaviour is essentially a three-step process:

1) Study and analyse what your consumers are actually doing (for example, which brands are they buying? When, how and where are they buying them?).
2) Consider why they are doing what they are doing (for example, is it because of some strong rational or emotional reason or a desire for status?).
3) Decide what you need to do in order to get consumers to consider doing what you want them to do.

So, how do we find out what consumers are doing? We conduct market research.

Primary and secondary market research

Market research is defined by:
1) The person or people who conduct the research.
2) The number of respondents who are researched.

As for who conducts the research, there are two options here: primary research and secondary research. Primary research is research that you design and conduct yourself. It can come in many forms, but what's important to understand is that you design the research, conduct it and interpret the research findings yourself. Secondary research is research that has already been conducted by a third party. When you hear news stories about ongoing political polls or large studies from companies such as MRI (Mediamark Research & Intelligence) or SMRB (Simmons Market Research Bureau), you can see information on media habits and market shares of brands where all the research has been conducted by a third party. For example, go to <www.mriplus.com> and register for free to gain access to thousands of pages of consumer research.

40   **The Fundamentals of Marketing**

⇐ The business of marketing
➜ **Consumer behaviour**
⇢ Product and brand development

The second question we must consider is, 'how many respondents are we going to approach?' All research is either quantitative (meaning that enough respondents were researched to make the research statistically reliable and for the results to be extrapolated to a larger population) or qualitative (usually featuring fewer respondents, but going into much greater detail).

For example, MRI+ quantitative research shows me that African Americans are nearly three times as likely to smoke menthol cigarettes as Caucasians. That's simply a fact. But why? To understand why African Americans in the US are far more likely to smoke menthol cigarettes, I would have to design qualitative research to dig deeper.

Probably the most important decision you'll have to make with respect to research is simply, 'what do I need to know?' Clearly stated research objectives will help guide your pursuit of knowledge. The worst thing you can do is to set out to find out everything you can. Living in the information age, you can easily bury yourself in information about a brand and possibly still not find out what you need to know. A quick googling of Coca-Cola nets 38 million responses. The googling of Google nets 2.6 billion responses. Obviously, you can easily become overwhelmed if you don't know exactly what you are looking for.

Begin with secondary research

Once you have determined what you need to know, the best place to begin is with secondary research. Generally, secondary research is quantitative and answers a lot of questions about your brand, category and competition without the huge expense of having to conduct this research yourself. It's fast, convenient and, with some excellent quality research firms doing the research, it's generally quite reliable.

Where can you look for secondary research? There are thousands of reputable research firms around the world. Consider government census data. This information can give you a tremendous amount of information about the demographic make-up of the population.

Industry trade associations can also provide a tremendous amount of information about buying habits, growth trends and much more. In addition, company's annual reports, public relations releases/files, technical reports and product registration forms can all give you a huge amount of information to get started.

[design ethnography is] **a way of understanding the particulars of daily life in such a way as to increase the success probability of a new product or service or, more appropriately, to reduce the probability of failure specifically due to a lack of understanding of the basic behaviours and frameworks of consumers.**
Tony Salvador, Genevieve Bell and Ken Anderson

Secondary research on the Internet

The Internet has created an explosion of available secondary research, much of it available free of cost. Try some of these sites.

Information topic	Web address
US government demographic information	\<www.census.gov>
UK government demographic information	\<www.statistics.gov.uk>
Financial and population statistics for the EU	\<ec.europa.eu/eurostat>
Industry/company information	\<www.hoovers.com>
Information on technology markets	\<www.forrester.com>
Category/brand case study information	\<www.WARC.com>
Directory of US research suppliers	\<www.greenbook.org>
Internet usage by country	\<www.internetworldstats.com>
Product category, brand and media information	\<www.mriplus.com>

Interpreting secondary research

Let's say that you are interested in the chewing gum business. Maybe you have a new chewing gum idea and want to find out who chews a lot of gum. According to MRI+, a heavy user is defined as chewing more than four pieces of gum per week. Roughly 30% of American adults fall into this category. Younger adults are more likely than older adults to be heavy gum-chewers with the 18–24 year old group indexing at 138 (meaning the average frequent gum chewer is 38% more likely to be in this age group).

A frequent gum-chewer is more likely to be female (index 111), work in sales or an office (index 119), make above $60,000/year, slightly more likely to live in the southern United States (index 103) and not the north-east (index 94), has never married (index 120), has a child in the household who watches Cartoon Network (index 122), Comedy Central (index 117) or the Disney Channel (index 122) and read magazines such as *Glamour* or *Seventeen* (both index 153).

42   **The Fundamentals of Marketing**

←← The business of marketing
➜ **Consumer behaviour**
→→ Product and brand development

That's not exactly a clear picture is it?

What we can take from this is that the act of chewing gum is a pretty normal one in the US with a very large population doing it regularly. With women more likely to chew gum than men, you'd think more companies would be trying to create chewing gum brands solely targeting women. Since the presence of children is also a predictor of chewing gum frequency, it may be important to create brands that appeal to both mother and child. If the mother is the buyer (or 'gatekeeper') for the child, we may simply want to appeal to the mother. This could lead us to create chewing gums that are good for your child, maybe with vitamins or fluoride, for example.

Secondary research often creates as many questions as it answers. For example, why do people stop chewing gum at middle age? Why are there geographic discrepancies in the amount of chewing gum used? Why are women who have never married far more likely to chew gum? Are there super-heavy users who chew more than four pieces each day instead of each week?

How will we learn the answers to these questions? We'll need to design our own research… primary research.

Observe your customer

I once worked on a feminine hygiene product with an ambitious brand manager who planned a major package redesign. The new designs looked fantastic; clearly superior to the old packaging. However, in observing women buying the product in a supermarket and several grocery stores, I observed that these customers were able to grab exactly the right box off the shelf without even looking at the shelf or slowing down even a little. If we did a major redesign of the package our loyal users wouldn't be able to find the exact box they wanted without stopping and comparing boxes. Feminine hygiene isn't a category that women want to study. They want to grab the right product and get on to the next item on their list. We therefore recommended baby steps on the package redesign. Our client disagreed vehemently, but when she viewed the footage we had of women shopping the aisle, she agreed to test her new product on-shelf. When the new packages were tested on-shelf, they confused our customers and business in that store decreased by over 30% that day. Observation can lead to great insight.

Designing primary research

When you control the research, you can design it any way you wish. There is simply no limit to the types of research you can conduct. Let's take a look at some of the major forms of primary research.

Try it!

Try your product. How do you like it? How do you think it compares to its competition? How would you make it better? While you don't want to be overly swayed by your own personal opinion, you don't need to ignore it either. David Ogilvy (1911–1999), often referred to as the father of advertising, is quoted as saying that the key to being a great advertising practitioner is to become an 'everyman'. In other words, learn to think as your target market does and you will be able to predict their reactions. Try out your brand as well as your competition's brand. Find out for yourself your product's strengths and weaknesses and those of your competition.

Get to know your consumers

Observation is one of the most powerful tools you have to understanding why people do what they do. Watch them shop for goods and services. Watch them use the products. See how they 'comparison shop' and how they shop differently in a supermarket from how they do in an upscale department store. The more you know about how your customer purchases and uses your brand, the better equipped you'll be to make good decisions on the brand's behalf.

Focus groups and one-on-ones

Get seven (or so) people in a room with a moderator to discuss their experiences and opinions of products and you have a focus group. Focus groups are one of the most popular forms of primary, qualitative research because they are relatively cheap to set up and you are hearing from a significant number of people. For this reason, most major manufacturers have consumer panel groups that are asked to comment regularly on everything a brand is doing. On the other hand, the one-on-one in-depth interview approach can get into much greater depth about a brand than a focus group can – for a rounded view it can be useful to employ a combination of both techniques.

Projective research

It is often necessary to move beyond straight questions and answers to get to the truth. Getting consumers to project their beliefs and feelings can be an effective way of seeing what they really think as opposed to what they think they should tell you. Market research firms will hire psychologists, anthropologists, sociologists and the like to design research to get at deep-seated beliefs. Purpose-driven games, photo sorts (where consumers are asked to categorise different images) and collage-building are all versions of projective research techniques.

Surveys and test markets

Whether it's snail mail, email or telephone, survey information can be very beneficial to understanding the big picture. Marketers will also often test market products and even advertising communications in small, localised campaigns prior to risking tremendous amounts of money by launching a product nationally.

> **Any communication or marketing professional needs cross-cultural research and communication skills to be able to succeed in the future.**
> Marye Tharp

44 **The Fundamentals of Marketing**

←← The business of marketing
➜ **Consumer behaviour**
⟩⟩ Product and brand development

Inventing the next Facebook

Does anyone remember Friendster? Friendster.com was one of the first online social networking sites in 2003. It quickly became the major player in social networking, gaining three million users in only a few months. Today, 90% of users are based in Asia. North Americans and Europeans have pretty much moved on to other social networking sites. The Internet moves at hyper-speed and staying on top requires constant innovation. After only about two years, Friendster was toppled by MySpace which was then toppled by Facebook. com; all within about five years.

So, if you wanted to invent the next market leader in social networking, how would you do it?

First you'd probably spend a lot of time gaining first-hand experience with all the major players (such as Facebook, MySpace, Friendster and Twitter). Once you understood the existing sites, you'd want to talk to people who love the sites and people who hate them (either in focus groups or one-to-one interviews). You'd probably hire some people to keep diaries of their social networking or get them to agree to allow you to observe them. Secondary research could help you determine demographic and psychographic profiles of the users. Quantitative surveys could help you understand what people like, don't like and still want in a social networking site. A literature review to see what the experts are saying about social networking could also help you find strengths and weaknesses.

In addition, trend research could help you predict where the social networking scene is going in the future. Bill Gates, founding partner at Microsoft, predicted the demise of the personal computer over a decade ago when he realised other devices would become smaller and far more portable than a computer could be. Smartphones (like Apple's iPhone) aren't merely supercharged telephones; they're the beginning of everyone having their full computer in their front pocket. So, what are the implications for social networking? Sure, Facebook has mobile applications, but what about a social networking site that is totally phone-based, which allows you to better organise all your online life, stay in closer touch with friends and employ voice recognition technology far more simply than any of the current products available?

You can always invent a better product. Always. But to do so requires an in-depth understanding of current products, strengths and weaknesses as well as future trends to see where the market is going.

Will Facebook go the way of Friendster? Probably. One thing is for sure: there are hundreds of people working on its replacement right now.

Don't take it at face value

Research is good. The misinterpretation of research is bad… very bad. Marketers who follow consumer research literally without question or comprehension are setting themselves up for potential disaster.

The Chrysler K-Car
In the late 1970s Chrysler made one of the biggest automotive breakthroughs of the 20th century. Their engineers figured out how to place a car's engine sideways (thereby taking up less interior space) and to make cars front-wheel drive. These changes gave consumers more interior room, better traction and a car of less weight, which led to dramatically improved fuel consumption. As America's perpetual number three car maker, this technological innovation was Chrysler's big opportunity to take market share from General Motors and Ford.

The mistake came in auto design. By using focus groups to help refine the car's design, they put consumers in charge of designing cars. They took everything consumers said quite literally and changed the design over and over until all they had left was a box. American consumers don't buy cars because of their technological advantages. Americans buy cars based on design. Chrysler introduced the K-car to a lukewarm response due to its boxy design. GM and Ford quickly followed in the technological advances but with better-looking models and got the advantage of Chrysler's innovation. Retired CEO Lee Iacocca said that after this mistake Chrysler would only introduce car designs that some people loved and others hated. The 'one size fits all' design philosophy at Chrysler was officially dead. And if you think about it, for all of Chrysler's ongoing business issues, they are among the most innovative designers in the world.

New Coke
In 1985 Coca-Cola was hurting from the Pepsi taste tests so they decided to do the unthinkable: change the hundred-plus year-old formula. Basically they made Coke taste like Pepsi. Why? Because in blind taste tests more consumers taking a single sip of both brands preferred Pepsi. The people at Coke took that at face value and reformulated Coke to taste like Pepsi. But did consumers really prefer the sweeter taste of Pepsi to Coke? On one sip yes, but when consuming an entire bottle or can, Coke drinkers prefer Coke. Everyone went out and tried new Coke, but hard core Coke drinkers rebelled. They liked old Coke better and they shouted it from the rooftops. Coke, trying not to embarrass itself, reintroduced old Coke as Coke Classic. They gained a small percentage of market share in the short term out of curiosity, but long-term the move was considered one of the biggest marketing disasters of the past century.

46   **The Fundamentals of Marketing**

←← The business of marketing
➔ **Consumer behaviour**
→→ Product and brand development

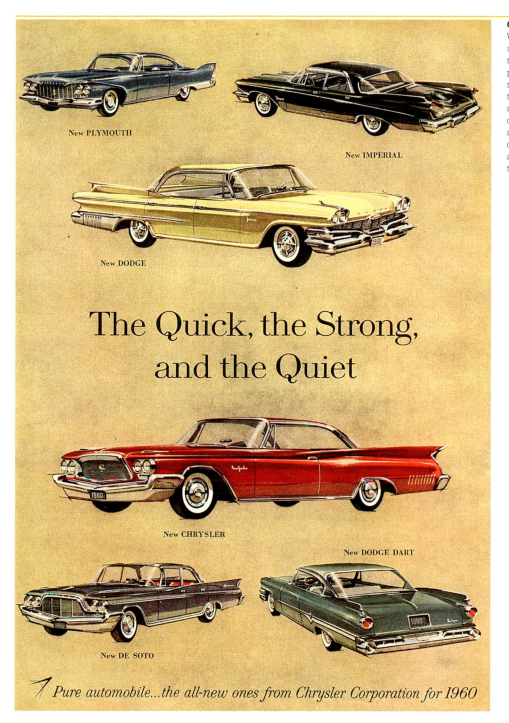

New PLYMOUTH

New IMPERIAL

New DODGE

The Quick, the Strong, and the Quiet

New CHRYSLER

New DODGE DART

New DE SOTO

Pure automobile...the all-new ones from Chrysler Corporation for 1960

Chrysler – Focus group design
When the designers at Chrysler started using customer focus groups to refine the look of their 1970s K-Car they produced a bland, boxy design – far removed from the sleek and stylish look they had established in the 1960s. By attempting to follow the feedback of their customers, without sufficient analysis or assessment, they missed out on a golden opportunity to exploit key technological advances to take market share from their competitors.

Consumer behaviour influencers

Understanding what consumers do is interesting, but it is only half the job. The really important thing to understand is why they do what they do. Once you understand why, you can begin to predict behaviour and in marketing, that means sales.

There are three basic influences on consumer behaviour:
1) Environment
2) Culture
3) The individual's psychological make-up

Environment and consumer behaviour
We are affected by everything around us: friends, family, advertising, trends, celebrities, prices, past experiences status and perceived status. All these factors add up to the environment in which we live.

Family life cycle

Another important part of our environment is our stage of life. This is known as the family life cycle and explains how people in a typical nuclear family move from complete independence to interdependence back to independence at the end of their lives

Bachelor stage

Young, single with no children.

Consumers in the bachelor stage have recently acquired their independence and acquired credit for the first time. As a result, they tend to spend freely, believing that they are entitled to everything their parents had plus everything they ever wanted that their parents didn't have. They have few limitations at this point, believing their entire lives are right in front of them for the taking.

Newly married couple

Young, two incomes and no children.

They are filling a home together with furniture, cars and such one-time purchases as silverware and cooking utensils. Generally, incomes nearly double as the two come together while expenses grow by only about 50% (as opposed to a single household) making for substantial discretionary income. Newly married couples often over-spend their means significantly (getting into considerable credit card debt) as they become accustomed to spending as a married couple.

Full nest one

Young married couple with youngest child under six.

Suddenly they nearly stop spending on themselves and begin spending on their child. Beyond clothing and baby furniture, there are music lessons, sports teams, and a further education savings account. Financial discipline usually starts developing out of necessity during this phase.

48   **The Fundamentals of Marketing**

← The business of marketing
➜ **Consumer behaviour**
⇢ Product and brand development

When you sit down for breakfast tomorrow, pour yourself a big glass of fresh, cold milk. Do you think anyone will look at you strangely? Then go to a hot new nightclub and order a glass of milk. Notice any difference? The environment dictates the appropriateness of your beverage selection. In one environment, your beverage selection is perfectly appropriate and in another it is completely inappropriate.

In much of the world, brands are seen as a demonstration of your success. Throughout post-communist Eastern Europe, even the poorest day labourer would have had a pack of Marlboro cigarettes to share with friends at a club. But Marlboro cigarettes were expensive in Eastern Europe. Most of the time, the box was filled with local brand cigarettes that cost a tenth the price. The status of the Marlboro package in that environment gave 'badge value' to the owner even more than the actual product.

Brands can tell others who we are, what we think and value, and even signal our level of success in the world. This all stems from the environment we live in and its effect on consumer behaviour.

In China in the late 1990s Western brands were displayed in people's apartments like art. A box of Kellogg's breakfast cereal would be prominently displayed to tell everyone coming through the house that this family was in the know and could afford expensive Western brands. As the environment in China changed, status symbols became increasingly important.

Your age and the generation you belong to have a huge impact on how you view the world, what you hold true and your belief structure. Gender, sexual orientation, family status, educational attainment, ethnicity, income, geography and occupation all play a major role in defining who you are, what you think, how you react and how you view the future.

Full nest two

Young married couples with youngest child over the age of six.

Children become more rather than less expensive as they grow older. Also, about this time, the parents are in need of a fashion refresher and their household appliances and furniture may be in need of replacement too. This can be a very expensive stage where it's likely there won't be enough money to go around. Credit plays a big role during this period.

Full nest three

Older married couple with dependent children in secondary and further education.

The children have reached their peak expense between their needs and wants. A child's further education is a huge financial undertaking for most parents. This is one of the most important times in a child's life so it's likely the parents are sacrificing to help their children as much as they can. Credit often gets used heavily again at this point.

Empty nest

Older married couple with no dependents.

Having successfully launched the children into lives of their own, the couple are facing retirement. They are likely beyond their peak earning potential and just trying to recover after paying for their children's education. Retirement may come any time between the age of 55 and 70 depending on the individual's health and the economic realities of available savings and the state of the economy. This is a time when the couple are likely to treat themselves to something they've always wanted such as a prestigious car. Credit usually gets paid off as the focus shifts to preparing for retirement.

Solitary survivor

Older single people.

Chances are one spouse has passed away leaving one person on their own. They may remarry or choose to go it alone from this point with a multitude of options. No matter which they choose, a common concern with senior citizens is whether the money they have saved will last as long as they do. With people living longer, the concern is legitimate. Either way, their expenses tend to move toward medical costs and away from personal indulgences such as clothing and travel.

← What is consumer behaviour?
→ **Consumer behaviour influencers**
→→ Consumer behaviour and psychological make-up

49

Culture and consumer behaviour

Culture is what defines a particular group of people at a specific time and place. It is the culmination of the knowledge, values and beliefs a group of people holds in common. Culture is constantly evolving and changing. Who we are, what we believe, what we want out of life, our view of justice, fairness, appropriateness are all the result of the culture we live in.

Countries have cultures and numerous subcultures within that larger culture. There are traits that are typically American, Russian, Japanese, Indian or whatever country you choose – but within each country are subcultures which make up the larger country culture. Ethnic cultures, demographic cultures and societal class cultures, which all have a huge impact on who you are, what you believe, how you act and react.

Basic geographic cultures change little over time. Consider the collectivist cultures of Japan and many other Asian countries that value the contribution of teams of people over the individual versus the individualistic cultures of much of the Western world that value the contribution of individuals over that of the team.

But these cultures do change. For example, consider the phenomenal changes in China and India. The closer these countries move to unbridled capitalism and the consumer-driven culture it inspires, the faster their individual cultures race toward a more individualist culture where your value as a human being is measured by financial success. So, is China an individualistic culture now? No. At its heart, China will remain a collectivist culture for many years to come. The unravelling of thousands of years of culture probably take at least hundreds of years to change, and may never change completely.

Culture directly affects consumer behaviour. Modern Western cultures such as the US tend to value what's new and what's next. As a result, products aren't built to last as the chances are they will be discarded for the next evolution or fashion update long before they have worn out. This doesn't only hold true for clothing and appliances; it even goes for the permanent things in our lives such as houses. America is one of the most mobile societies in the world with the average American having nearly eight different homes during their lifetime. By contrast, in Germany they have a saying that when you are building your home, you are building it for yourself and your great-grandchildren.

50   **The Fundamentals of Marketing**

←← The business of marketing
→ **Consumer behaviour**
→› Product and brand development

Marketing to the global audience

Marketing to a global audience is simply marketing to a local audience multiplied by the number of countries your product is sold in. If you make the assumption that the Chinese or Indian consumer will like your product for the same reasons and use it in the same way as a German or French consumer you are likely to lose big time, or at least not win at the level you could have if you'd targeted each market individually.

Despite this, marketers like global brands. The idea that you can sell one product to more than six billion people with the same packaging and advertising gets accountants all excited. Some brands have succeeded, such as Marlboro, Coke, Intel, Microsoft and Nokia.

But other brands require substantial adjustment from market to market. A laundry detergent full of bleach may deliver ultra-white clothing in a market obsessed with cleanliness, but in an environmentally concerned market or a market where drinking water is hard to come by, this may be a huge disaster.

Understanding a culture takes time, along with trained professionals to break down the belief systems and help us understand how we are similar and how we differ. To market outside your home country, you have to understand the people, the market and the competitive set-up in as much detail as you did when you became a success in your home country. There are no shortcuts here.

German McDrive

When McDonald's introduced the Drive-Thru in Germany during the early 1990s, cars were lined up and down the Autobahn. The German customers would drive in, order, pick up their food and drive to the side of the road. They would then stop by the side of the road, set up a table and chairs from the trunk of the car and eat their meal. At that time, Germans simply wouldn't eat in their cars, and certainly not while doing something as serious as driving. That was disrespectful to safety, to the car and also the meal. That thought probably never occurred to any American. It's a funny story now, but it shows the effect a culture can have on a marketing idea.

← What is consumer behaviour?
→ **Consumer behaviour influencers**
→→ Consumer behaviour and psychological make-up

51

Consumer behaviour and psychological make-up

Are you a risk taker, or do you prefer to watch from the sidelines? Do you define success as the accumulation of great financial assets, or your contribution to society? When Sony introduces its next technological breakthrough, will you order in advance sight unseen, or wait until year two when the price comes down and the bugs are all worked out?

Your psychological make-up is unique to you and goes a long way to defining what kind of consumer you are. Your attitudes, personality, psychographic make-up (lifestyle characteristics such as interests and opinions) and your lifestyle all have a tremendous impact on who you are as a consumer.

There are many secondary studies that segment people by their behaviours (for example VALS – values, attitudes, lifestyles) to help predict consumer behaviour based on the kind of person you demonstrate yourself to be. VALS group consumers into eight different groups: 1) innovators, 2) experiencers, 3) strivers, 4) achievers, 5) believers, 6) makers, 7) thinkers and 8) survivors.

Needs and wants

What kind of consumer you are is often dependent on your reasons for purchasing a particular product or service. For example, are there rational reasons, emotional reasons or status reasons?

We all have basic needs as human beings: clean air, water, food, clothing and safety. In most of the Western world fulfilling these basic needs for survival is not all that difficult. Thus, about 98% of what we see in our shopping malls is not about fulfilling physical needs, but satisfying psychological wants.

And not all wants are created equally. In 1943, Abraham Maslow wrote a paper entitled *A Theory of Human Motivation* that yielded Maslow's famous Hierarchy of Needs, as seen in Figure 2-1.

> **Behaviour in the human being is sometimes a defence, a way of concealing motives and thoughts, as language can be a way of hiding your thoughts and preventing communication.**
> Abraham Maslow

52   **The Fundamentals of Marketing**

←← The business of marketing
→ **Consumer behaviour**
→» Product and brand development

Hierarchy of needs

Moving from bottom to top, we begin with physiological needs: air, water, food, the very basics of life. The next most important are safety needs: protection from harm, security (that which keeps us from risk). The third level involves a feeling of belonging and love; both are basic human needs to which we all aspire. Certainly one-to-one human contact leads the way here, but consider also how modern society has included such things as instant messaging, blogging and social network groups on the Internet all as ways to experience belongingness. Esteem is the next rung of the hierarchy. As humans, we crave some level of admiration for who we are and what we've accomplished in life. The final rung is 'self-actualisation', where we have reached the highest level of self-accomplishment and fulfilment that we can as humans. This is a level to which we strive and may or may not actually achieve.

So, what does this have to do with marketing? Products and brands try to fulfil different levels of this hierarchy.

Let's look at an example. Evian is water, a basic necessity for survival. So Evian is appealing to your physiological needs. Correct? To a man dying of thirst Evian fulfils a physiological need, but Evian water isn't generally purchased by dehydrated people near death. You can fulfil a physiological need with tap water. Is it safety? We know Evian is pure? Probably not. Most of us in the Western world have access to safe drinking water.

Evian probably appeals to our need for belonging. We're part of a group that drinks only the 'best' water. Our water must be brought all the way from France. It sounds a bit silly when you read it here, but watch people in a convenience store rationalising their exotic water purchases.

Similarly, why do you think iPod earphones are white? For decades, black earphones that blended into what the listener were wearing were the norm. Apple had to go out of their way to produce white earphones. If you want to belong to a smart and innovative group, those little white wires had better be running down the front of your shirt.

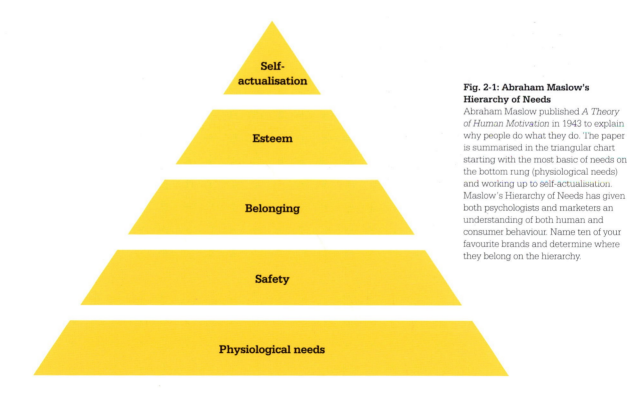

Fig. 2-1: Abraham Maslow's Hierarchy of Needs
Abraham Maslow published *A Theory of Human Motivation* in 1943 to explain why people do what they do. The paper is summarised in the triangular chart starting with the most basic of needs on the bottom rung (physiological needs) and working up to self-actualisation. Maslow's Hierarchy of Needs has given both psychologists and marketers an understanding of both human and consumer behaviour. Name ten of your favourite brands and determine where they belong on the hierarchy.

←← Consumer behaviour influencers
➡ **Consumer behaviour and psychological make-up**
→→ Market segmentation and target groups

53

Market segmentation and target groups

There are an infinite number of ways to segment your target audience to find the group best suited to your brand. Each segment is a group with different desires and beliefs. One of the most frequent mistakes marketing communications companies make is to determine their market segment and then act as if these people believe in the same things they do. 'Don't confuse yourself with your target', a research professor of mine used to say daily. It's excellent advice worth repeating.

The only products that truly appeal to everyone are clean water and air. Beyond that, products appeal to target groups: smaller segments of the population as a whole that have a need or want for the brand you are marketing. Identifying and getting to know your target consumer is critical to success in marketing. Some brands are successful in appealing to very large groups of consumers such as Coca-Cola or Pepsi. Others can be very successful in appealing to a very narrow group of people. Consider brands such as Tiffany jewellery. Tiffany has a very narrow select target group, but is a highly successful and profitable brand.

Marketers stereotype, they have to. Even in this age of nearly one-on-one communications, marketers rely on their ability to gather groups of like-minded individuals together to promote to. For example, older people are more set in their ways and less likely to try new products or new ideas. Women spend more money than men. Of course, this doesn't mean every older person is brand loyal, or that every woman spends more than every man, but the statements are broadly true for these sub-segments as a whole. For a stereotype to take shape, there is often a fundamental truth to at least some of what's being said. However, stereotyping can become an issue if we rely on it too heavily and don't do our homework to understand it. For example, in the US Asians have incomes 22% higher than the average American. But what do we mean by Asian? That covers an entire continent made up of Japanese, Chinese, Indonesians, Malaysians, Filipinos, Vietnamese, Burmese and many others. Are they all 22% wealthier than the average American? What about first generation vs second-generation immigrants? Is one wealthier than the other? As you can see, relying on a stereotype or broad statistic, without understanding what's behind it, could send you in the wrong direction.

You can segment the population in thousands of different ways. To put this into context, let's take a look at some of the more common market segments.

54   **The Fundamentals of Marketing**

⇐ The business of marketing
➡ **Consumer behaviour**
⇢ Product and brand development

Opinion leaders

A society will always have opinion leaders who are generally the first to try new products, help set trends and be very valuable to brands trying to get established. Opinion leaders are often show-business idols, politicians or sports stars. When Michael Jordan started wearing Nike, everyone started wearing Nike.

When Red Bull was first introduced in the US, Red Bull refrigerators were taken to movie shoots and given away free to cast and crew for years before the first consumer got the opportunity to have the energy drink. Once a generation of movie stars had adopted the beverage, there was no stopping Red Bull, the number one energy drink in America.

At the moment, the weight opinion leaders carry appears to be diminishing in the US (but certainly not disappearing). Consider fashion. What is in style today? The answer, probably for the first time in history, is everything. Everything is in style right now. Whatever you want to wear is in style. Why? Because teens of today don't feel the same overwhelming need to mimic others outside their peer group as they have in the past. Armed with YouTube and a host of ways to become famous themselves, these teens are confident enough in themselves to make their own rules and one of those rules is to not be manipulated by marketers or celebrities.

> **A rich man is not just a poor man with more money. He has different ideals, different personality forces, different church membership, and notions of right and wrong all stemming from social class differentials.**
>
> Pierre Martineau,
> *Motivation in Advertising*

Subcultures

Every country has a unique culture and then a variety of subcultures which when added up become the dominant culture of the country. The subcultures can be geographic, demographic or psychographic in nature. As an example, let's take a look at some of the subcultures in America.

Ethnic cultures

The largest ethnic group in America is Hispanic, which makes up 14.5% of the population or 42.7 million individuals. This is also the youngest group with a median age of 26 compared to 35 for the general population. But Hispanics are not simply Hispanic; they're Mexican, Puerto Rican, Cuban, Dominican, Spanish and come from dozens of Central and South American countries. While they may have a common language, there are different dialects, different food preferences, different customs and cultures.

Marketers have long been interested in reaching Hispanic cultures given their larger families, higher brand loyalty and tendency to spend a higher percentage of their incomes on food, clothing and beauty aids than the average American. Reaching them just means making your commercial in Spanish, right? No, not exactly. What they really want is the same thing we all want: respect for themselves and their culture.

The second largest ethnic group is African Americans, who make up 39.7 million or 13.4% of the US population.

African Americans are a group growing in affluence and influence. Today, over 80% of African Americans over 25 years old hold high school diplomas (up from 51% in 1980), 17% have completed college (up from 8% in 1980) and over one million hold advanced degrees. While their median income still lags behind the average American ($31,285 compared with $43,318), they are increasing at a faster pace.

Asians are one of the fastest-growing and most affluent demographic groups in the US. There are 14.4 million Asian Americans or 4.3% of the US population. Their personal income is 22% above the national average. They are the best educated of all groups being 75% more likely to have graduated from college than the national average.

The most obvious subcultures revolve around ethnic and racial differences. America is known as a melting pot immigrant nation containing every different race and ethnicity in the world. In the older cities, such as Boston and New York, these racial and ethnic groups tend to live together. For example, in New York City, Harlem is African, Chinatown and Little Italy are obvious, parts of Brooklyn are Russian, other parts are Irish and still other parts are Orthodox Jewish. But subcultures also include any demographic or psychographic breakdown you want to make, such as gender, religion, age, occupation or geography. All are subcultures within any country or society.

←← The business of marketing
→ **Consumer behaviour**
→→ Product and brand development

Social class

Like every society in the world, from the very privileged to the destitute, America has a class structure that affects consumers and marketers.

The upper-upper class, which represents 0.5% of the population, is 'old money'. This is at least second-generation wealth of locally prominent families. Their goals are to uphold the family name, to live graciously and to reflect well upon their breeding. As consumers, they purchase little. Most of their belongings are inherited within the family and the upper-upper class generally feels no need to try and prove or display their wealth.

The lower-upper class (1.5% of the population) is considered the *nouveau riche* or newly rich. These first generation multi-millionaires and billionaires have made their vast fortunes themselves. Their goals are a combination of gracious living and a drive to continue succeeding and acquiring even greater wealth. As consumers, all their possessions are new. They acquire prestige through acquisitions. They purchase more than any other single group by far.

The upper-middle class (10% of the population) is considered moderately successful. They tend to be management-level executives or owners of medium-sized businesses. Their goal is career success and as consumers, they tend to reflect that success in their home décor and social and cultural participation. They want badly to be part of the upper class and will work feverishly to try to achieve that level of wealth. Like the lower-upper class, most of their high-prestige possessions are new.

The lower-middle class (30–35% of the population) is largely made up of small-business owners and highly paid blue-collar workers. Their major goal in life is to be accepted and live a respectable life. As consumers, they tend to be more conservative, not needing to show off their money but rather save and prepare for their children's future. Their most important goal is for their children to graduate from college (which only about 28% of the American public does).

The upper-lower class (40% of the population) is made up of semi-skilled production-line workers and retail workers. Their goal is enjoying life and living well day-to-day (or pay cheque to pay cheque). As consumers, they generally strive to be 'up with the times' and fashionable though they are usually followers of fashion, not leaders. The upper-lower class tends to feel some degree of uncertainty about their future so they tend to buy heavily on impulse and probably owe quite a sum of money on their credit cards.

The lower-lower class (15–20% of the population) is the unskilled worker, unassimilated ethnic group and the sporadically employed. Despite making up 15–20% of the population, they make up only 7–8% of the purchasing power. These are the working (and non-working) poor. As consumers, they live pay cheque to pay cheque, buying almost totally on impulse and credit when they can get it.

We live in a culture where knowing your customers one by one as individuals is more important than ever before. Large mass demographic trends are no longer as predictive as they once were because the marketplace is too diversified.
Ross Goldstein

← Consumer behaviour and psychological make-up
➜ **Market segmentation and target groups**
⟩⟩ How people shop

57

Demographics

We can segment our audience by demographic characteristics such as sex, age, religion, political view or lifestyle. Virtually any group you can think of can be a legitimate target audience. Let's take a look at some of the obvious ones in America.

Women are not a minority; men are. Women make up 50.9% of the population but control 75% of the discretionary spending in the US. The vast majority of advertising shown on television and in print targets women for this very reason.

Consumers over 50 years old account for approximately 30% of the US population. This baby-boom generation controls 55% of discretionary spending and 70% of the net worth of the entire population. With statistics like that you might think that everyone would be targeting baby boomers. However, this target demographic tends to be set in their ways and less likely to adopt new brands than their children. Also, even with a median net worth of US$466,000, their biggest fear is that they will outlive their money.

Some marketers are taking notice of the GLBT (gay, lesbian, bisexual, transgender) market because of its size. GLBT accounts for approximately 6.5% of the population and is the single highest buying power of any minority group. But be careful. While these four different demographic groups often get lumped together, the reality is that few products hold particular interest to all four groups. For example, Subaru has found that their Forester SUV has a special attraction to lesbian women and Jaguar appears to be especially attractive to gay men. There aren't many cars more different than a Subaru Forester and Jaguar so it would be inaccurate and misleading to say Subaru appeals to the GLBT community, when in fact they appeal to the 'L' community.

Bottom line? If you have a specific target or brand that appeals to certain members of the GLBT community, understand exactly, to whom you are appealing so you can target your messages accurately and specifically.

The age of mass marketing is dead – it's inefficient and too expensive. The next step is finding applications of existing products to very niche groups. About a year ago, much fuss was made about the gay market – now it's singles.
Simon Sinek

←← The business of marketing
→ **Consumer behaviour**
→→ Product and brand development

Malvern Water

Malvern is a small English country town. This advert for Malvern spring water emphasises its traditional, rural origins while simultaneously courting the gay community and giving the brand a contemporary spin.

'Malvern is a registered trademark of Atlantic Industries

malvern. not quite middle england.

malvern. *the Original* ENGLISH NATURAL MINERAL WATER

STILL

Since 1851

←← Consumer behaviour and psychological make-up
→ **Market segmentation and target groups**
→→ How people shop

59

How people shop

Have you ever bought a car? If so, it will likely be one of the most expensive purchases you will make in your lifetime so you probably researched different car brands, shopped around, took test drives and argued about the price. How does the way you buy a car compare with the way you buy milk? Chances are you simply go to the store and if the price seems fair you buy the milk. You don't shop around, taste it first and barter over the price of milk in the same way you do a car. How do you buy a hair cut? If it's just a trim, you will probably just go to wherever is closest; if you are having a completely new style then you might go to the salon with the best reputation.

All three are purchases, but the buying behaviour behind them is very different. Some purchases require a lot of research, some require none. Some require shopping for the best price, some require shopping for the best service no matter what the price may be. Every purchase is different.

Northwestern University took a look at how people shop for groceries and found that (in the US) they spend an average of 12 seconds per product category. That's right! If you want to sell your target consumer a new brand of pasta sauce, you have 12 seconds from the time they enter that section of the store until they have made their selection and moved on. Why is this important? It's easy to believe that consumers go through great angst in making every decision. They don't. They don't have the time or the desire to make anything any more difficult than it has to be. As a marketer, it's important to respect how consumers make their decisions and work within that decision-making process. Northwestern University also found out that 85% of shoppers only picked up one brand, 90% only picked up one size and 58% paid attention to the price before placing the product in their shopping cart (which, of course, also means that 42% paid no attention to the price).

Predicting consumer behaviour

Cynics and entrepreneurs refer to market research as a 'view through the rear-view mirror'. It's true that research will tell you how the world is at a given point in time and nothing more. Marketing changes at the speed of light and marketing managers that become overly dependent on 'what the numbers say' are unlikely to ever create major successes. The key is learning to actually predict future consumer behaviour.

For example, this pressure cooker world we live in has added a tremendous amount of stress to our everyday lives. Assuming stress continues to mount, what do you think that will mean for the vacation/holiday business? What types of vacations are we likely to want in ten years? Does it actually involve travelling or not? Will we take shorter vacations of fewer long vacations? Do we want to be surrounded by our friends, anonymous in a crowd of strangers or completely alone? Knowing the vacations people are taking today is only one small piece of information in the decision of what to plan for in the future.

Since ultimately your job in marketing is to 'sell stuff', learning to predict consumer behaviour is critical to your overall success. It's not only critical; it's something the marketing industry is generally not very good at. Every year in the US roughly 12,000 new products are introduced. Of this, roughly 2,000 will succeed and an astonishing 10,000 will fail. That's right, 75–80% of new products fail in their first year. This is literally hundreds of millions of dollars thrown away every year because someone wasn't very good at predicting consumer behaviour.

There are four major reasons new products fail:
1) It was simply a bad idea in the first place.
2) There's a flaw in the marketing mix.
3) Someone misunderstood the research.
4) Trends have changed.

Let's take a look at what drives each type of failure in order to try and avoid these pitfalls as we put together our marketing plan for the Smart Battery.

Simply a bad idea in the first place

One of the funny things about product failures is that most of them seem completely absurd after the fact. Did the people at Pets.com actually believe people would order dog food online, wait for it to be delivered in a week and pay shipping that could increase the cost by 50%? It is worth noting that Pets.com is now owned by a different, and much smarter, company.

R.J. Reynolds Tobacco Company spent $300 million on the launch of Premier smokeless cigarettes. That's great; finally a satisfying smokeless cigarette! And who wants a smokeless cigarette? Non-smokers of course. Smokers actually like the smoke – that's why they smoke. Non-smokers love the idea of smokeless cigarettes, but since they don't smoke, they didn't buy them. This was simply a bad idea for the target audience of smokers.

Want some Crystal Pepsi? That's right, Pepsi-Cola that is clear. Nope? Neither did anyone else. Just because you can do something doesn't mean you should.

I notice increasing reluctance on the part of marketing executives to use judgement; they are coming to rely too much on research, and they use it as a drunkard uses a lamp post. For support, rather than for illumination.
David Ogilvy

← Market segmentation and target groups
→ How people shop
⇶ The Everyman effect

61

Flaw in the marketing mix

This can be a very broad topic since it covers everything from product problems to pricing problems to distribution issues to target market issues to advertising and promotion issues. For example, Sony once had a product called Betamax. It was a video cassette recorder that was clearly superior to the VHS format. So why did it fail? The main reason was that Sony patented Betamax technology so that only they could produce Betamax machines. This meant that other manufacturers were forced to produce their machines in the inferior VHS format. This led to competition among the VHS market, which in turn led to lower prices and greater availability of recorded materials. This one poor decision of patenting the technology meant that although Sony had a clearly superior quality product they still experienced a spectacular market failure.

Similarly, Microsoft's ZUNE MP3 player has a number of superior features to Apple's iPod (such as file sharing). However, the design isn't as nice, the promotion doesn't make it as 'cool' to own and as a result, Apple controls more than 80% of the MP3 market.

Ever seen a product that costs too much – or too little? We'll go into depth on this in Chapter 4, but finding the optimum price is as critical to success as product design or advertising. How about a product without adequate distribution? A few years back, Red Bull introduced Full Moon bottled water (water only bottled during a full moon). Red Bull is a fun brand and I suspect Red Bull lovers would have purchased it if they could find it, but weak distribution meant that they couldn't get hold of it and the idea was scrapped.

And finally, too little or too much advertising and promotional support can kill a new product. Promote the brand too little and retailers aren't going to support or even carry the brand. Advertise too much and consumers will likely think there must be something wrong with the product that you have to advertise it so much.

How do we avoid flaws in the marketing mix? Research and honest interpretation of the research. There are testing methods available for every part of the marketing mix that will help you to optimise your plan.

Misunderstanding the research

Cynics of marketing research will tell you that research can be designed to prove anything you want in marketing. They are right. However, that doesn't mean we should stop researching. The key is to research honestly and be prepared for answers you don't want to hear. It's difficult to have consumers tell you that you have a bad idea, but if it's a bad idea, better to find out now than several millions of dollars from now.

As we saw on page 46, the classic story of misunderstanding research has to belong to the Coca-Cola company for its introduction of New Coke back in 1985. Pepsi had been eating into Coke's market share for years with the Pepsi challenge. In blind side-by-side taste tests more people preferred Pepsi (which is a sweeter formula) to Coke. Coke was still the market leader, but clearly worried. So, New Coke was introduced to the world. Everyone tried it; it was big news that Coke had abandoned their 100-year-old secret formula for this new formula. But Coke drinkers rejected it. Despite what the research said, Coke drinkers were buying Coke because they preferred the taste to Pepsi's sweeter formula. Within weeks, Coke Classic was back on the market and the company was trying to look like they had done this on purpose.

←← The business of marketing
➜ **Consumer behaviour**
→→ Product and brand development

Trends change

For decades General Motors had been making increasingly larger and more powerful vehicles (such as pick-up trucks and sport utility vehicles). Despite the pressure on oil prices and increasing concerns about their environmental impact, every year the cars seemed to get larger and fuel economy actually got worse in many circumstances. In the summer of 2008, fuel prices around the world rose beyond all expectations. One of the largest companies in the world, GM seemed to be completely out of touch with car buyers. But were they?

In the US, over 50% of vehicles sold are light trucks meaning sport utility vehicles and pick-up trucks. Add to that the fact that SUV sales had grown consistently for nearly two decades, the top one and two selling vehicles in the US are both pick-up trucks and car manufacturers have always been able to make greater profit per vehicle off pick-ups and SUVs, and it's easy to see why General Motors, Chrysler and Ford have spent so much effort on light trucks over traditional cars.

However, with fuel prices becoming increasingly unpredictable, light truck sales declined sharply. Trends change and there is usually some tipping point that changes everything. In the US, that tipping point appeared to be fuel prices, war and energy dependence. That said, at the time of writing, fuel prices have declined once more and newspaper stories abound with news of surging SUV sales. We'll see.

High gas prices are going to revolutionise the way we drive and move our society to more fuel-efficient vehicles. Unfortunately, it's taken a crisis of high gas prices to move us in that direction.
Bill Richardson

←← Market segmentation and target groups
→ **How people shop**
→→ The Everyman effect

63

The Everyman effect

Marketing done well is all about understanding people's hopes and dreams and helping them fulfil both their wants and needs. Let's take a look at 'selling' a candidate for President of the United States.

Political elections

The key to getting elected in a democratic society isn't experience, education or in many cases even ideology. The key to getting elected is convincing voters you are similar to them; you understand what they care about, you are concerned about the same things and you share their beliefs. If we hired our leaders the same way we hire people for jobs, few of our leaders would be in power.

In 1992 Bill Clinton, governor of the small and relatively unimportant state of Arkansas, took on one of the most experienced politicians of our time, then President of the United States, George Herbert Walker Bush. George Bush Sr. had been a lifelong public servant as head of the CIA, Vice President under Ronald Reagan for eight years and President for four years. How do you get a more

perfect career history than that? Looked at critically, it seems absurd to think a 'nobody' with little relevant experience could come along and take what should have been Bush's second term right away from him. However, watch some of the 1992 debate footage and you'll see Bill Clinton coming off as the Everyman who 'feels your pain' and cares about what you care about. Asked the price of a gallon of milk, George Bush had no idea. Clinton could tell you the name of the shopkeeper where he bought his milk.

Fast forward to the 2008 US Presidential election; John McCain had a lifetime of experience while Barack Obama had substantially less. If you hired by experience, you'd hire John McCain. However, in an interview McCain couldn't recall how many homes he and his multi-millionaire wife Cindy owned (the correct answer was ten). Barack Obama overcame lack of experience, almost no federal government experience, race, name recognition and about every other possible disadvantage because people could see hope in his 'American-dream' story. Son of a poor emigrant father, raised by a single mother, works hard, goes to

the very best schools in the US, forgoes high-paying jobs to give back to the inner-city black community, gets elected at a state level, then national level and becomes President of the United States. If he can, maybe I can too.

And John McCain wasn't the only one Barack Obama defeated. He also defeated Hillary Clinton, thought to be a guaranteed shoo-in for the job. But Hillary Clinton didn't have that same Everyman quality her husband was so very good at displaying.

How do you get elected President of the United States? By understanding people and more importantly showing that you are one of them.

64   **The Fundamentals of Marketing**

⇐ The business of marketing
➜ **Consumer behaviour**
⇝ Product and brand development

On the campaign trail
Barack Obama's Everyman qualities
helped him to win the most powerful
position in the world.

Case study: Amazon.com and analytics

Amazon.com knows that I love Celtic music and suggests new artists I might like, allows me to sample their albums and links me to even more artists I might never hear about any other way. Similarly, when I bought Al Gore's *An Inconvenient Truth* DVD, Amazon began suggesting environmentally friendly cleaning products, energy-efficient light bulbs and more. But they offer even more than that...

I encourage my students to buy textbooks from Amazon Why? Because you almost never pay full price and you even get an option to buy used versions from a variety of sellers. This guarantees you get the best product at the best possible price. And that's what Amazon is all about: an online consumer-centric store where customers can find anything they want at the lowest possible prices.

How do they do it?

How does Amazon know me so well? Analytics. Analytics is the new buzzword for tracking consumers' viewing and buying habits, compiling a profile of each customer in order to predict future behaviour. Amazon's computer program tracks everything I do on their site (cyber-observation). That's not unusual, but they've taken it a step further in order to use that information to recommend other products and services they believe I might like as well.

In a world of fewer and fewer true product innovations and less product superiority, marketers are turning to analytics to get to know their consumers better and therefore better serve their needs. For example, let's take a look at Internet radio station Pandora, which creates a radio station based on the user's favourite artists or songs. Pandora's Music Genome Project dissects a song using 400 different attributes to try to match it to songs that have been composed with similar themes, similar instrumentation, similar vocal styles and so on. The station then streams music of a similar genre allowing the listener to hear new music and new artists they are predicted to like. And it works.

←← The business of marketing
➔ **Consumer behaviour**
→→ Product and brand development

If this works so well for music, what else might it work well for? Books? DVDs? Electronics? Food items? Cosmetics? Clothes? Sports equipment? What wouldn't it work well for? Companies such as Procter & Gamble, Netflix, Capital One Credit Cards and thousands more are getting into the business of statistically analysing their consumers in order to better predict their future wants and needs.

Analytics can also increase the value of each sale. For example, I recently heard a Celtic harpist named Aine Minogue on Pandora.com and decided to buy one of her CDs. I was able to click right on the 'Buy CD at Amazon' button and go directly to the CD. The CD was listed at $16.98. In addition, Amazon put together three of her most popular CDs (since they know I have never ordered any of these before) for the low price of $50.94 (note, that is merely $16.98 times three). Below that they tell me that customers who bought Aine Minogue's CD also bought CDs from Enya, Lorenna McKennitt and others. That tells me other music I'm likely to want. I can sample every song on the CD and buy it as a CD or an MP3 download. There are three more attempts on the page to introduce me to similar artists and lists of similar music. Amazon.com has turned the search for a single CD into a musical education on Celtic harpists with many options to sample and buy products aimed directly at me.

Moral of the story
The better you know your customer, the better you can serve them and the more loyal they will become. Amazon started business in 1995 and is the largest retailer on the Internet. Why? Because they know their customers better than anyone else. They know what they buy and what they reject largely through their use of consumer analytics. While compiling consumer analytics is nothing new, the ability to use that information to make real-time product recommendations is a relatively new phenomenon and one that every serious marketer has to look at as a way to build their business going forward. We are creatures of habit. We like what we like and don't like what we don't like. If marketers can efficiently compile that knowledge, they can actually make marketing as consumer-focused as it claims to be.

amazon.com.

Dear Customers,

The American Customer Satisfaction Index is, by far, the most authoritative and widely followed survey of customer satisfaction. Last year, Amazon.com received an ACSI score of 84, the highest ever recorded -- not just online, not just in retailing -- but the highest score ever recorded in any service industry. This year, Amazon.com scored an 88 -- again the highest score ever recorded in any service industry.

In ACSI's words:
"Amazon.com continues to show remarkably high levels of customer satisfaction. With a score of 88 (up 5%), it is generating satisfaction at a level unheard of in the service industry...Can customer satisfaction for Amazon climb more? The latest ACSI data suggest that it is indeed possible. Both service and the value proposition offered by Amazon have increased at a steep rate".

Thank you very much for being a customer, and we'll work even harder for you in the future. (We already have lots of customer experience improvements planned for 2003.)

On behalf of everyone at Amazon.com,

Sincerely,

Jeff Bezos
Founder & CEO

Amazon top 'The American Customer Satisfaction Index'
According to The American Customer Satisfaction Index (ACSI), an independent assessor of US consumer opinion, Amazon.com leads the way in online customer satisfaction. ACSI reports scores on a 0–100 scale and in 2001 and 2002 Amazon scored the highest ever customer satisfaction rating (84/100 in 2001 and 88/100 in 2002). These were the highest recorded scores for any company in any service industry. At the end of 2008 Amazon dropped two points to 86/100 – but still remains one of the strongest exponents of customer satisfaction in the world.

←← The Everyman effect
→ Case study: Amazon.com and analytics
→→ Smart plan: Part two

67

Smart plan: Part two

Consumer behaviour and your marketing plan

In this chapter we reviewed the value of understanding and predicting consumer behaviour. The way to do this is through market research and that begins with an analysis of your brand's situation in the marketplace. You are therefore about to begin collecting a tremendous amount of information to create what is called a situation analysis for your Smart Battery.

The situation analysis is a research-based understanding of a brand's status in the marketplace at a given time: where we are and why we're there. This will give us the foundation to know what we should do next. Most marketers begin their annual marketing planning with the development of a situation analysis so they can gain a shared understanding of the brand's strengths, weaknesses and opportunities for the future.

The situation analysis outline

→ First of all, the category analysis involves gaining an understanding of how the battery category (not any specific brand) is performing over time. This includes category history, structure, sales regionally, sales seasonally, pricing history, distribution history and promotional spending.

→ Secondly, your brand analysis should include information on your brand's history, structure, sales regionally, sales seasonally, pricing history, distribution history, promotional spending and research knowledge summary.

→ Competition analysis is an understanding of how your main competitors are doing in the marketplace. The competition analysis includes your competitor's history, brand structure, packaging analysis, research knowledge summary, sales regionally, sales seasonally, pricing strategy, distribution strategy and promotion.
  In the competition analysis, promotion covers advertising, sales promotion spending, public relations spending, personal selling.

→ SWOT: a SWOT analysis is the summary of a situation analysis showing strengths, weaknesses, threats and opportunities.

Smart Battery: Exercise two

Using the above outline, write your research objectives (what you want to learn), and your research strategies (how you will learn that information). Then, using the information included in the chapter, do your secondary research and design and conduct your primary research for understanding the battery consumer, the product category, the retail environment and the competitive situation. You may not be able to find all the information listed above, but find as much as you can.

68   **The Fundamentals of Marketing**

←← The business of marketing
➔ **Consumer behaviour**
→→ Product and brand development

Chapter questions and exercises

1 Define and explain consumer behaviour.
2 Choose two different product categories (for example, a high-interest product such as ice cream and a low-interest product such as baking flour) and observe at least 30 people shop and choose a product. What have you learned about how people shop? What do they appear to care about? What don't they appear to care about? Are there different kinds of shoppers? How would you categorise them?
3 Explain the difference between primary and secondary research.
4 Discuss the differences you have observed in people of different cultures. Why do you think these differences exist?
5 Explain how and why marketers stereotype people.
6 Where do these brands fit on Maslow's Hierarchy of Needs? Sony, Victoria's Secret, Coach, Prada, Nike, Virgin Airways, Ben & Jerry's ice cream, Corona beer, Kia, Coca-Cola, Cadillac, Dell computers.

Product and brand development

Just a glass of water?
Would you like a glass of water? What kind? Water that falls from the sky or water that comes from under the Earth. How about a bottle of water? Mineral water? Spring water? Purified water? Water with gas (carbonated) or water without gas? Do you have a favourite brand? Maybe you have a favourite country you like your water from. How did this all get so complicated… after all, it's just a glass of water. Or is it?

Product and brand development are the foundation of your marketing programme. Until you have something to sell, all the other 'P's' are just words. Product development includes every tangible and intangible part of the product: how your product looks, tastes, smells and works as well as its level of quality, the quantity you sell it in and what it will and won't do. Brand development takes a product and distinguishes it from its competition and adds value.

Chapter 3 will help you:

→ **Learn how products are turned into brands.**
→ **Learn how to grow existing brands.**
→ **Position your product in the consumer's mind.**
→ **Develop new products and brands.**

Brands and branding

According to the American Marketing Association, a Brand is a name, term, sign, symbol or any other feature that identifies one seller's good or service from those of other sellers. The word 'brand' comes from the Norwegian *brandr* meaning to burn, as in branding cattle.

The difference between a product and brand

A product is something created by labour that can be marketed or sold as a commodity. A brand is created when you take that product and give it special meaning through names, logos or any form of identification that separates one seller's goods or services from their competition.

Why do we create brands? Quite simply, we create them because brands are worth more money than products. Brands are created from products, but not every product inspires a myriad of brands. Consider these commodities:

wool, cotton, cattle, chicken, soybean oil, wheat and metals (such as copper and steel). All are products, few are branded. Other commodities such as coffee are sold to companies that roast them differently, flavour them and turn them into some of the most valuable brands in the world. Think of a product as the tangible item itself and the brand as the intangibles that surround the product to differentiate it and make it special in consumers' eyes.

Product classification: Durable and non-durable

A durable good is an item that is normally used over and over again – such as a car, a refrigerator, a camera, clothing or household tools such as a pair of scissors. They are generally purchased infrequently and have smaller advertising budgets than non-durables (with the exception of very expensive items such as automobiles). A non-durable can be used only once – such as all food items or magazines. These items are normally heavily advertised because they are purchased with such regularity.

Making a brand

Are all brands distinctive? Not all. If you choose, you can buy a branded product as a commodity or near commodity. Many nationally branded products sell millions of units at a lower profit per item than speciality products that sell thousands at a significantly higher profit per item. These are two ends of the spectrum and there are hundreds of other brands that fall somewhere in between.

> **I don't think I am an actress. I think I've created a brand and a business.**
> Pamela Anderson

72   **The Fundamentals of Marketing**

← The business of marketing
→ **Product and brand development**
→→ Strategic pricing

People can be brands. Consider Tiger Woods, Michael Jordan, Bono, Barack Obama, Pope John Paul II or the ultimate branded person of all time: Oprah Winfrey.

If we hear Johnny Depp is in a new movie, the power of his brand will fill cinemas even before the critics have commented on the movie. Even more impressive is that Depp's brand is so powerful, chances are box office sales will be strong no matter what the critics say. The idea of people as brands was first understood by sports stars followed by entertainment stars and finally by politicians.

Branding is all about the creation and development of the brand, what it stands for and what it means to consumers. Coming directly out of this idea is brand management. Brand management is simply the act of managing all the elements of a brand's marketing mix. It was invented in the 1950s when companies began to compete with themselves with multiple brands in a single category. For example, when Procter & Gamble, the creators of brand management, wanted to introduce a new toothpaste to compete with their market-leading Gleem toothpaste at the time, they looked for different benefits, different target audiences and different ways to take business from Colgate. Crest was born and has been so well-managed you can barely find Gleem for sale any longer.

People brands
Oprah Winfrey is a very well-managed brand. You know what Oprah stands for and she remains consistent with her message of hope. What other brand qualities does she project? Describe her brand.

Managing and growing existing brands

When 19th-century multimillionaire John D. Rockefeller was asked how much money is enough money, he famously answered 'just a little more'. And so it is with your brand's sales. Marketers dedicate themselves to making their brands larger and more profitable year upon year. But how? Is there no limit to how high is up?

There isn't a single brand in the world that doesn't have even greater potential for growth. There never will be. You can always find new markets, new consumer groups, and new ways to build your brand. Sometimes the goal is a larger share of the business, sometimes a larger per item price or profit. You can increase sales, decrease sales, and increase price, or cut costs to boost profits; there are as many ways to increase sales and profits as your imagination will allow.

Brand management

By now you've probably noticed how literal we are in marketing and realised that brand management is likely to be about managing brands.

So, how do we manage brands? Each brand manager is given relatively free reign to manipulate their product, pricing, distribution, promotion and audiences targeted in a way to maximise their brand against their competition; even when some of the competition is owned by the same company.

Brand management has given way to category management in that most companies no longer introduce brands that compete head-to-head, but instead sell brands targeted at different consumers and different consumer needs.

74   **The Fundamentals of Marketing**

← The business of marketing
➜ **Product and brand development**
⟶ Strategic pricing

Brand extensions

When a brand introduces a new product under their brand name, this is referred to as a brand extension. The extension carries the halo of the mother brand's qualities into a new market. For example, Ajax is a popular powdered cleanser made by Colgate-Palmolive around the world. The brand is respected as an excellent cleaner and good value. What else could Ajax put their brand name on? They already have dishwashing liquid and floor cleaner. Could Ajax introduce speciality cleaning products for the bath tub, toilet and sink? What could Ajax do in the kitchen? Could they offer antibacterial cleaning for food preparation? How about dust removal products? What about products to remove oil stains in your garage? If Ajax means 'good cleaning' it could probably be successful with all these and more. Ajax laundry detergent? They tried once, but maybe it's worth doing again.

The technique worked for Kellogg's when they introduced new flavours of Special K (for example, fruit and yogurt) as well as Special K Snack Bars and Special K Bites and even Special K Protein Water with which they successfully took their weight-loss positioning into new areas. These were successful because they were consistent with Special K, its reason to be and quality.

However it is worth remembering that brand extensions aren't always successful and can even damage the position of the mother brand with its customers. For example, when Saab introduced the small hatchback 9-2, and the SUV 9-7, as brand extensions, consumers assumed that they would have the typical Saab quirky design and high quality. Unfortunately, instead of building a small hatchback and SUV from scratch, Saab took the less expensive route of adapting the Subaru Impreza into the Saab 9-2 and Chevrolet Blazer into the 9-7 SUV. Saab enthusiasts immediately recognised that these weren't true Saabs by the placement of the ignition switch (Saab puts them in the centre console; these have it in the steering column). Neither extension has been successful as a result.

Procter & Gamble's brand management

Today, P&G compete with themselves with nine separate brands in fabric care: Tide, Cheer, Dreft, Ivory, Era, Bold, Gain, Bounce and Febreze and up to a dozen line extensions within some of these brands. Ideally, each of these brands is attracting a somewhat different consumer looking for different things in their laundry soap. Brand management and category management allows the company to attract more consumers than any of its competitors.

←← Brands and branding
→ **Managing and growing existing brands**
→→ Why are brands important?

75

Brand positioning

How do we keep the hundreds of thousands of brands straight in our heads? It's called positioning. Your brand's position refers to where it fits in the consumer's mind.

Positioning was created by Al Ries and Jack Trout when in 1972 they authored the business best-seller *Positioning, the Battle for Your Mind*. *Fortune* magazine has referred to positioning as the 'most important business strategy of all time'.

A Volvo is a 'safe' car, a Honda is a 'reliable' car, and a Porsche is a 'well-designed' car. On that last example, some of you might be thinking, Porsche is a 'fast car'. You aren't wrong. A brand's positioning is where that brand fits in your head. Consumers determine positioning, not marketers. Marketers may decide on a positioning they want and try to figure out how to get it, but ultimately it is the consumer that positions the brand in their mind.

Why is positioning so important? Over-stimulation and clutter. For example, American consumers are exposed to nearly ten times the number of commercials as the average citizen of the world. They deal with this over-saturation by forgetting 85% of all they hear. Advertisers need to understand this and intentionally place their products in consumers' minds in a strategically smart place. Also, positioning should be done in relationship to something the consumer already knows.

Positioning statements

A positioning statement is a written statement that shows where you want to be in your consumer's mind. If you want to accomplish your goal of getting a place in your consumer's mind, keep your positioning statement simple. Remember, the only reason the concept of positioning exists is because of our over-saturation of information.

A successful positioning statement tells the consumers how to think about a brand and where to place it in their mind.

Occasionally marketers will use a selling line or slogan in their advertising that is also a positioning statement. When you can do this, it's a great way to solidify your positioning – here are some of the most successful:

→ BMW, the ultimate driving machine.
→ Mercedes, engineered like no other car in the world.
→ Built Ford tough.
→ We try harder. Avis
→ The world's favourite airline. British Airways
→ Have it your way. Burger King
→ Reassuringly expensive. Stella Artois Belgian Beer
→ Takes a licking and keeps on ticking. Timex watches
→ NBC, Must See TV
→ 1,000 songs in your pocket. iPod Nano
→ Nationwide is on your side

To establish a favourable and well-defined brand personality with the consumer the advertiser must be consistent. You can't use a comic approach today and a scientist in a white jacket tomorrow without diffusing and damaging your brand personality.
Morris Hite

76 | The Fundamentals of Marketing

←← The business of marketing
→ **Product and brand development**
→→ Strategic pricing

Positioning statements for beer drinkers

Blind taste tests show over and over that beer is beer is beer. And yet consumers do have very strong preferences for one beer over another. Why? Positioning. Where you put these beers in your mind plays a huge part in which you order in public and at home.

→ Corona Beer is a vacation in Mexico
→ Coors is the Rocky Mountain beer
→ Molson is the Canadian beer drinker's favourite
→ Heineken is a sophisticated European ('German' even though it isn't) beer
→ Amstel Light is Heineken's light beer
→ Budweiser is the all-American beer
→ Guinness is the taste of an Irish pub
→ Yuengling is the original American beer

Brand contacts

Brand contacts are any ways in which a consumer comes in contact with a brand. So, for a fast-food chain, that includes everything from advertising to the cleanliness of the stores to the efficiency and friendliness of the staff and of course, the quality of the food. Smart marketers try to control every brand contact to give consumers a consistent and positive message about the brand. For example, imagine if you were to walk into an official Nike store and it was stocked like a Best Buy discount store. Sound funny? That's because it's off brand strategy. The Nike store is one of many brand contacts that the company must constantly manage and maintain. As can be seen in Figure 3-1, brand contacts must be managed across a range of environments and situations.

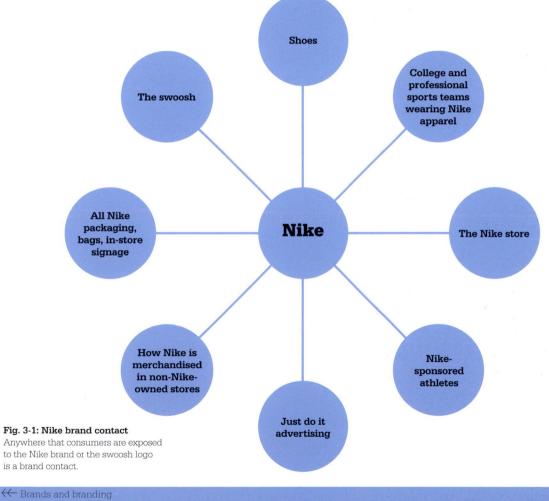

Fig. 3-1: Nike brand contact
Anywhere that consumers are exposed to the Nike brand or the swoosh logo is a brand contact.

←← Brands and branding
→ **Managing and growing existing brands**
→→ Why are brands important?

77

Brand loyalty

No matter what the brand, you will have some customers who are consistently loyal and buy only your brand. They're known as brand-loyal users. You'll have others who will use your brand some or even most of the time, but you can't count on them for every purchase. These are occasional users. You'll have other customers who will buy your brand only on rare occasions. These are infrequent users. Some will try your brand and reject it for some reason. Those we call 'tryer-rejectors'. And, of course there will be some potential customers who will never try your brand for whatever reason. These are non-users.

Why do we care about brand-loyal users? Because, generally about 20% of your users will make up 80% of your sales (it's called the 80/20 rule). In this case, these are probably the brand-loyal users who no matter what, will buy only your brand. These are your new best friends and you need to treat them with respect and care. It is far more cost-efficient to keep a loyal customer happy than it is to acquire a new customer who may eventually prefer one of your competitor's brands.

Brand equity

Marketers measure consumers' attitudes toward many attributes of their brands, both tangible and intangible. Brand equity is made up of the attributes your brand 'owns'. As shown in the box opposite, Volvo is seen as the safest car on the road whether it is or not. This is where perception becomes reality. Of course you never fully own an equity; you rent it. As long as your brand delivers better than your competitors do, and you are supporting the equity with every brand contact, that equity will likely be attributed to you.

For example, BMW owns 'fun to drive'. They support that attribute in advertising, product design and every brand contact they have. Smart brand managers know exactly which equities are important to own and make sure they are supporting them. Pantene owns 'shiny, healthy-looking hair.' Herbal Essence owns 'great scents'.

Brand equity is important for many reasons. Certainly consumers are more likely to buy products they believe in, but in addition to this the brand's value to the consumer also increases with a strong brand equity, making consumers more likely to pay more for the brand and less likely to be swayed by a competitor.

> **He goes by the brand, yet imagines he goes by the flavour.**
> Mark Twain

78   **The Fundamentals of Marketing**

←← The business of marketing
→ **Product and brand development**
→→ Strategic pricing

Brand personality and brand essence

Like people, brands tend to have very distinct personalities. These personalities come from communications, brand experience and the brand's history. IBM has a very serious personality. Dell is personable. Apple is cool. These 'personality adjectives' make up the brand essence.

Brand personality, or essence, can be important as you communicate and innovate your brand. If you've built a strong brand, you will want to keep one, consistent voice speaking for the brand. For example, IBM shouldn't try to be silly; it could actually hurt the brand. Identifying your brand personality and delivering that consistently will give you a more cohesive brand that consumers can count on.

Volvo's positioning

Volvo made the strategic decision not to compete on styling, typically an American attribute, or reliability, typically a Japanese attribute. Everyone wants their car to be safe, and superior safety can even compensate for less contemporary design, lower gas mileage and even a bit on reliability. Volvo's safety is legendary. In Sweden where the car is made, engineers and designers used to visit the location of every Volvo crash to study how the accidents occurred and how injury could be further avoided. Volvo has consistently demonstrated the safety of their cars for decades.

So Volvo is the safest car on the road, correct? Not exactly. Tests in Europe rated the Audi as a safer car, because its weight, acceleration and steering allowed the driver to avoid the accident in the first place. But Volvo continues to own 'safety' in consumer's minds.

If you wanted to compete directly with Volvo, how would you do that? Audi could do it as an even safer car, as a car that not only provides the crash safety of Volvo, but more contemporary styling.

←← Brands and branding
→ **Managing and growing existing brands**
→» Why are brands important?

79

Why are brands important?

As we stated earlier, brands are worth more than products. There is no chemical difference between the generic acetaminophen (also known as paracetamol) and brands such as Panadol or Tylenol, but most of us are willing to pay more for the branded product. This is true for nearly every product category. If you've ever bought a bottle of water, you've demonstrated that.

Why are brands worth more to us than products? There are many reasons. Consider the US pain-killer Tylenol: why do so many people buy it when the generic product is much cheaper and equally effective?

→ We know it works; it comes from a large, very successful company (Johnson & Johnson) so we can easily believe it has been tested and perfected.
→ Many people will actually tell you they believe the acetaminophen/paracetamol in Tylenol is a better quality than is used in cheaper generic products.
→ The advertising reassures us that Tylenol is the best.

I know that the active ingredient used in the generic capsules is the same as in the branded capsules. What do I buy? Tylenol.

There are hundreds of reasons why people choose brands over unbranded products. Brands assure, they empower, they demonstrate wisdom, they convey status and about a hundred more adjectives.

Value of brands

The idea of brands being more valuable than products became evident about 20 years ago when investment bankers began spending substantially more to buy brands than the sum of manufacturing facilities, marketing facilities and so forth was worth. This was the birth of people beginning to study and understand brand equities in relationship to real money.

Many companies have developed methods to value brands, however the most widely used process comes from a company headquartered in Switzerland: Interbrand PLC. They developed a system that measures seven criteria to establish the value of a brand.

(right) Interbrand's brand valuation
Interbrand's seven criteria for measuring brand strength and assigning a dollar value of the brand. Each section is given a maximum point value to show its relative importance.

80   **The Fundamentals of Marketing**

←← The business of marketing
→ **Product and brand development**
→→ Strategic pricing

Every year *Business Week* magazine and others publish the Interbrand findings of the most valuable brands in the world. So, what are the most valuable brands in the world? Some of the 2008 list may surprise you. Students generally assume their favourite brands are among the most valuable in the world, and while they may be to you, according to Interbrand, Nike is #29, Apple is #24, VW is #53, Amazon.com is #58, and Starbucks isn't in the top 100. Note that most of these brands are much newer than the top ten and are likely still in their strong growth phase.

Brand	Interbrand value
1) Coke	$67.0 billion
2) IBM	$59.0 billion
2) Microsoft	$59.0 billion
4) General Electric	$53.1 billion
5) Nokia	$35.9 billion
6) Toyota	$34.1 billion
7) Intel	$31.3 billion
8) McDonald's	$31.0 billion
9) Disney	$29.3 billion
10) Google	$25.6 billion

Brand strength criteria	Explanation	Maximum point value
Market	How strong is the market this brand competes in? For example, cigarettes are a shrinking market while computers are a growing market. The emphasis is on the market, not your brand in that market.	10 points maximum
Stability	Is your brand well known and well established in its market?	15 points maximum
Leadership	Every category has a share-leader as well as a thought-leader. It's not enough to just be the largest brand in the category; is your brand leading the category in innovation and influencing the entire market?	25 points maximum
Internationality	Is your product available internationally or could it be? International sales can help keep a brand stable. When sales are down in one region, they may be up in another.	25 points maximum
Trend	Is your brand on an upward sales trend? This is not about being 'trendy', which can be terrible for a brand as it's hot one day and gone the next.	5 points maximum
Support	Is the brand consistently supported in marketing communications at strong levels?	10 points maximum
Protection	Is the brand protected legally from competitors' ability to copy the product?	5 points maximum.

←← Managing and growing existing brands
→ **Why are brands important?**
→→ Developing new products and brands

81

Developing new products and brands

New products and new brands are the growth engine of every successful marketer. However, with a failure rate upwards of 80%, managing new product development is both costly and risky. Most brands start with someone inventing a new product (void of consumer input). Someone invents a new product and then people from marketing or sales are sent to figure out how the new product should be sold.

There is certainly nothing wrong with product innovation. We should lead consumers when we can. How could anyone have known they needed an MP3 player before the technology was invented and they could experience 1,000 songs on something the size of a credit card? Someone had to figure out what was possible.

New to the world products

Every good marketer has a research and development team simply trying to solve problems. Just because no one has found a cure for the common cold doesn't mean that a) there isn't one and b) there aren't thousands of people working on the project each and every day. There are.

Ask any consumer about their favourite brands and eventually they will come up with problems they wish would be fixed. We are never really satisfied with 'good enough'.

We want 'better, different, more' from everything we buy.

Look at all the diseases that still have no effective cure. Even something as simple as human obesity is likely to be curable one day with a product that is currently unknown. Engineers and inventors are constantly looking for ways to improve our lives through better products, more efficacious products and even a few things we haven't yet thought of.

New products/brands are created under one of three research and development (R&D) processes:
1) Consumer-led R&D
2) Technology-led R&D
3) Opportunity-led R&D.

Consumer-led R&D

Once you have got to know your consumer, you can figure out products and brands they love and hate. Understand what they love so you can duplicate it and figure out what they hate so you can improve upon it.

Ideally new products fulfil some consumer want or need. Simply study your consumers' habits and find products they want or need where you can either create something new or create something better than whatever product is currently fulfilling that need.

82   **The Fundamentals of Marketing**

← ← The business of marketing
→ **Product and brand development**
→ → Strategic pricing

Women in the US report that the number one stress they face every day is figuring out what they should prepare for dinner. It's not a particularly difficult task, but done every single day, it can be tedious and time-consuming. What ingredients do we have on hand? How can I use them to create some variety without trying to use new recipes all the time? How would you solve this problem? Kraft Foods, the world's second largest food company, has websites where you can input ingredients and they will suggest recipes. In the near future, ingredients will be monitored electronically with potential recipes available with whatever you happen to have on hand. You'll simply click on your phone and options for dinner will appear. Will that lessen women's daily stress?

Not all consumer-led R&D is so problem/solution-focused. No one asked for the iPod. We didn't want it or need it. But, we did want everything it represented: freedom, music anywhere, high-quality sound, everything we owned musically in a very compact form. This type of consumer-led R&D looks at consumers' desires and tries to find new ways to give them what they really want, even if they can't see the possibilities for themselves.

Most new products are a variation of something that already exists, a combination of two or more products or a new use for an existing product. Have you ever heard of a Grapple? It's what happens when you cross a grape and an apple. It has the form of an apple, but smells and tastes like a grape. Actually, it's grape juice/flavouring shot into an apple; see <www.grapplefruits.com>. I doubt any consumer asked for their apple to taste like a grape, but they probably talked about how much they loved apples and grapes and someone got the great idea that we could sell two commodities (apples and grapes) at a premium price.

Even an iPod is simply a computer mass storage device. It has nothing inherently to do with music. Anything you can store on a computer can be stored on an iPod. Apple took someone else's technology and branded it a music player, then a video player.

What else could you make out of a computer mass storage device? How about loading books on them? How much paper could be saved by simply loading books on to thumb drives that can be read on your computer, or telephone for that matter? You could sell books, movies, newspapers or TV shows. All we've done is combine one technology, the mass storage device, with another, books and movies, and we have an entirely new product (just check out the Amazon Kindle e-reader to see what's already possible).

Let's drive not just breakthroughs in new products, but new ways to give more and more people access to these inventions and their benefits. This is a broad and important mission, and I believe we all have a part to play in it.
Bill Gates

← Why are brands important?
→ Developing new products and brands
→→ Organising for new product development

83

Technology-led R&D

Many companies simply set R&D engineers the task of creating new technologies and find uses and target groups for them later. Consumers can't express a need or want for a product they can't imagine. Someone has to invent it and explain it.

Take Swiffer from Procter & Gamble. No consumer ever said they wanted an electrostatic cloth with small holes that would trap dust and remove it better than sprays. How could they even imagine any such device before Swiffer was introduced in 1999? Today, 50 million homes around the world have fundamentally changed the way they dust furniture because technology-led researchers invented the product and marketers figured out how to maximise its potential.

Three years earlier, P&G researchers figured out how a liquid in a spray bottle could encapsulate odours so that you couldn't smell them. The odours (often caused by bacteria) are still there, your nose simply can't perceive them once they have been sprayed with Febreze. Again, no one in a focus group said 'I wish I could encapsulate odours in a spray so that I can't smell them.' However, once the product was introduced to us, many families found a pressing need for it.

Opportunity-led R&D

Once someone creates a successful brand, they have also created opportunity for competition. How many computer brands do we have all doing essentially the same thing? How about phone companies? Once Red Bull was introduced in its native Austria and began to gain a following, competitors came from everywhere to cash in on this new phenomenon of energy drinks. Some promised better taste, some simply larger cans, some trendier names (such as Cocaine, Rock Star or Monster), some offered new forms (such as 5 Hour Energy, which ironically comes as a small tonic; Red Bull's original form).

The US has nearly 200 brands of cold breakfast cereal. As a result, the largest brands in the category have less than 5% market share and most brands have less than 1% market share. However, once Kellogg's got us eating prepared cold cereal for breakfast, the opportunity was there for the taking.

Satellite TV has 500 channels, satellite radio has 200 channels, there are over 5,000 magazines and a billion websites. Opportunity creates opportunity and whenever a new technology or product type is invented you can be assured someone will be waiting to take advantage of it.

Global product adaptations

The other common way that brands are created is through taking a product or brand available in one part of the world and introducing it (or rebranding it) in a different part of the world. That is exactly what happened with Red Bull. Red Bull was the reformulation and rebranding of an energy tonic used in Thailand mostly by factory workers to help them get through long shifts. Reformulated and rebranded, it created the fastest-growing drink segment in the US for about the last decade. There are countless opportunities on store shelves around the world waiting to be discovered.

Let's create a brand

Let's work with a new product idea that isn't available on the market (hint, go manufacture this and you could make millions). One of my first jobs in marketing was working on Trident Sugarless Gum for then owner Warner-Lambert. 'Four out of five dentists recommend chewing sugarless gum for their patients who chew gum' the advertising would repeat over and over. Many consumers thought we were saying dentists recommended chewing Trident, which simply wasn't true. It got me thinking, Trident was advertising that they aren't bad for your teeth. What if they could advertise that they are actually good for your teeth?

I started reading dental research, asking research and development people and consumers what it would mean to have a chewing gum that was actually good for your teeth. I found out that research in the UK had proven that chewing gum after a meal actually removes 85% of the plaque removed by brushing. That's impressive, but toothpaste also contains fluoride. Could a chewing gum contain fluoride?

I conducted consumer research on the topic and found almost universal acceptance, even enthusiasm. I next checked with our global sales force and found out that there is a fluoride chewing gum in Portugal. We got a case sent to us and did more research. Again it was nearly 100% positive.

It's a great idea still, so let's imagine we're creating the brand right now – here are some of the questions we will need to answer:

- What will we call our fluoride chewing gum?

- What is our positioning statement for the new fluoride chewing gum?

- What size and shape should it be?

- What should the packaging look like?

- Who is our target market?

- What flavours should we introduce?

- Where should we sell it?

- How much should we charge for it?

- How should we promote it?

- What other brands are its main competitors and how is it different or better than they are?

←← Why are brands important?
→ **Developing new products and brands**
→→ Organising for new product development

85

Organising for new product development

There are five basic steps to new product development. With each step taking greater manpower and financial resources to accomplish it is important to weed out as many average or poor ideas as possible early on. The five steps are:
1) New product ideation
2) Concept testing
3) Product in use testing
4) Market testing
5) New product introduction

New product ideation

Armed with a strong understanding of their consumers, groups of marketers will get together to brainstorm potential new product ideas. Usually a professional moderator will guide their discussion and help them to come up with as many good ideas as possible. Participants usually include brand managers, advertising people, consumer research professionals and occasionally new product ideations will be done in partnership with consumers.

The moderator will normally come up with a problem that needs to be solved. For example, carbonated soft drinks are losing popularity with the current generation of teenagers. Develop soft drink ideas targeted directly at this group. The ideation group will have several prompts that will remind them of the interests of this age group to help them develop more and better ideas.

When they are done, the group will normally choose the best 10–15 ideas on their own (probably out of the hundreds developed). The next step will be to show the ideas to consumers to get their reaction.

Product concept testing

Marketers determine whether or not to pursue new product ideas based largely on something called concept testing. A product concept is a short description of a new product with a simple drawing of what that product might look like. Consumers are shown the product concept and then asked their opinions of the ideas in the concept and ultimately asked about their interest in purchasing the product.

←← The business of marketing
➜ **Product and brand development**
→→ Strategic pricing

Product concepts are normally tested in either one-on-one situations with a moderator or in focus groups. Once qualitative information is accumulated and the concept is fine-tuned, it will be sent to about 10,000 respondents either through traditional mail or email so that quantitative data can be collected.

If the product concept is considered a success (in relation to other successful brands tested), the next step will be to make prototypes and test the product in consumers' hands.

Product in use test

The winning concept(s) from a product concept test will then be assigned a team of people representing marketing, finance, R&D and advertising to turn a concept into reality.

The R&D team will go off to develop a prototype of the product in order to get it into consumers' hands. Consumers will try or use the prototype product and make comments meant to improve the product along the way. The marketing people will work on developing the ideal marketing mix of product, price, distribution and promotion. They will name the brand, create all the elements of the branding (such as logos and packaging). The advertising team will begin to work on communications strategies and finally the finance team will develop plans for how to pay for the brand's introduction.

The point of this step is to get qualitative feedback from consumers actually using the brand so we can make whatever adjustments necessary before a quantitative test is begun.

An Apple a day… Apple's life cycle

Apple introduced its first iPod in October 2001. It's only eight years later at the writing of this book, and the sixth generation of the iPod Classic is for sale, the fourth generation of the iPod Nano (first introduced in 2005), second generation of the iPod Shuffle (also introduced in 2005) and the second generation of iPod Touch (first introduced in 2007). To date, there have been 44 different iPods introduced (not counting the variety of colours).

My original iPod from 2002 still works just fine, but it's been replaced five times by newer even more fashionable models. That's right, the iPod is fashion and as such must come in and go out of style. The technology got only a bit better, but the colours changed, they got smaller, they got larger memories, they became video players, they got celebrity endorsements and the list goes on and on. iPods changed like fashion and so far Apple has done an amazing job of keeping us engaged with the brand.

Most companies would have been happy just to introduce such a product and would still be selling the same product introduced in 2001. Apple saw much larger potential in making the iPod into a fashion statement and continually upgrading and changing just so we would all collect them. To date, approximately 165 million have been sold.

←← Developing new products and brands
→ **Organising for new product development**
→→ Case study: Petstages

87

Market testing

The next step is to place the brand into the market under as realistic conditions as possible. Will consumers buy it? How often? How many will buy it multiple times? How fast can we expect the brand to grow? How long will it grow for? The goal is to get quantitative data that tells us how our entire marketing plan will work and to determine whether or not to actually introduce the brand.

This can be done by placing the brand in full distribution in a few well-chosen markets that are representative of the greater country you plan to introduce in. Ideally, you want a substantial-sized population with isolated media you can run advertising on without the entire country seeing it. We refer to these as test markets.

Test marketing can be very difficult and expensive so research companies have developed pre-packaged testing programmes that guarantee better control of distribution, shelf presence, pricing, daily sales figures and advertising tracking. One such company available in most of the world is IRI Behaviorscan®. Behaviorscan allows you to place products in various markets to test their viability prior to introducing on a regional or national basis.

In the online world, this market-testing is usually called beta-testing. Internet users are invited to use the new product in exchange for their comments and help in perfecting the product.

As with any testing, market testing helps us to learn and perfect our marketing plan to maximise its impact when the product is finally introduced more widely.

New product introduction

Assuming you have passed your concept test, product-in-use testing and your test market, it's time to determine how you will introduce your product to the general public. Few companies have the resources to introduce products across an entire country at once, supported with a substantial promotional campaign that may not pay out (break even profit-wise) for three to five years. More and more we are seeing pay-as-you-go funding that expands into a large enough area to become profitable with a smaller investment and expansion as it is affordable.

New product introductions require a tremendous amount of strategic thinking. Some products are introduced only to opinion leaders who will help spread and disseminate news about the brand. Clothing designer Tommy Hilfiger is famous for giving clothing away to inner-city trend starters and watching the brand spread like a virus. Tylenol introduced their products in hospitals alone until they could refer to it as the number one choice of hospitals. Red Bull gave the brand to Hollywood starlets in the music and movie business for years ahead of selling the first can in the US.

Once you've decided to go forward with a new product introduction, production must be planned, the sales force has to plan how to build adequate distribution, pricing will probably be adjusted somewhat as you negotiate with retailers for space, and everything will be perfected based on what you learn along the way.

88   **The Fundamentals of Marketing**

←← The business of marketing
➜ **Product and brand development**
→→ Strategic pricing

Product/brand life cycle

Most products (and brands) go through a four step bell-shaped growth known as a product life cycle. New products tend to start their growth curve slowly, attracting only the innovators in society. Once the innovators adopt a product, the early majority sets the brand into a steep growth curve. Once the brand peaks in sales, the late majority takes over and sales commonly begin to dip. Finally the laggards adopt the product and it either goes along steadily or will be in some level of decline.

While this is the classic product life cycle, as you can imagine, marketers work hard to avoid having their products dip in sales too early.

Fig. 3-2: Product life cycle
The classic product life cycle illustrates how brands are adopted. Marketers try to keep the growth curve going up by introducing new versions of the brand (such as new flavours or colours) or by making improvements to the basic product.

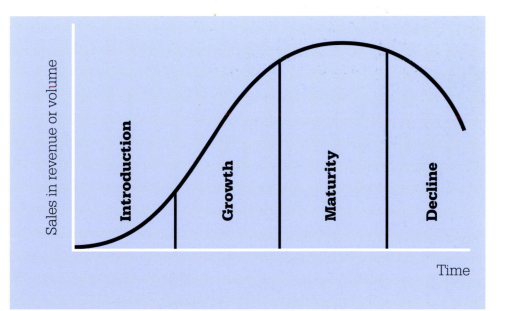

← Developing new products and brands
→ **Organising for new product development**
→→ Case study: Petstages

89

Case study: Petstages

We love our pets, but how much do we think about their happiness? How much do we think about their development? Does a new puppy have different needs from an old dog? Do dogs have different needs during the day for stimulation, soothing, chewing or playing? It only makes sense – right?

So when was the last time you took a good look at your pet's toys? Are they exciting and colourful or dull and boring? You do love your pet, right?

Introducing Petstages' developmental toys for your pet
Petstages creators Torjus Lundevall and Mariann Straub are entrepreneurs who look for opportunities to improve products or entire product categories.

For example, after painting a few rooms in her home, Ms Straub realised she only used a paintbrush once and then just threw it away. The paint store manager assured her that most amateur painters do exactly the same thing. Think about that. If you are buying a paintbrush for a single use, you are likely to buy the cheapest and lowest-quality paintbrush you can, and probably one that does an inferior job. So,

Ms Straub invented a single-use paintbrush with an ergonomic handle and screw-off throw-away brush. Now amateurs can use a professional-quality paintbrush, perfectly contoured to their hand, and still throw away the brush end without guilt. Doesn't that make perfectly logical sense?

When Mr Lundevall and Ms Straub looked at the pet toy market, they saw marketers not paying much attention to the needs of our beloved family pets. The product quality was generally low; the products were ugly and cheap. In developing the Petstages concept of targeted toys for each stage in your pet's life, they also had their own personal experiences as pet owners to draw on. Certainly a four-month old puppy has very different needs from a 14-year-old 'senior' dog. It makes perfect sense.

So, once the two business partners got the vision for what they wanted to create, they consulted with veterinarians about the different needs and stages of pets' lives, they hired baby-toy designers to develop bright, beautifully designed toys and developed a full line of pet toys to provide animals with stimulating, soothing, interactive and playful toys in bright colours. Products with purpose.

←← The business of marketing
➜ **Product and brand development**
⇒⇒ Strategic pricing

The current product line has over 100 different products aimed at dogs and cats. The dog products address dogs' chewing needs with 27 toys, interacting needs with six toys, playing needs with four toys and soothing needs with seven toys. There is also a separate line of 14 toys specifically targeting the needs of miniature dogs. All are produced in fun, bright designs and are higher quality than most dog toys on the market. They also cost around twice the price of an average dog toy.

Petstages has expanded internationally, selling in more than 20 countries throughout Europe as well as North and South America and are in the process of introducing a new line for dogs called Occupi. The Occupi toys contain treats, which the dog has to work out how to get at.

Now a few of you cynics are thinking… 'Aren't dogs supposed to be colour blind?' Hmmm, maybe the dog isn't the only target market for these toys. Maybe the buyer is the real target here…

Moral of the story
Great opportunities often lie in overlooked areas and it is often worthwhile asking how you could improve a product; any product. Walk through any store and look at different categories of products and then think about how you could improve upon the products in that category. For example, in most industrial countries the senior citizen market is growing faster than any other and yet the products aimed at this market are often painfully out of date and of terrible design and quality. It is also worth imagining different ways to make your very favourite product better. I once asked a class of 17 students to agree on a single favourite product. It was their iPods. They felt it was perfect in design, functionality and reliability. I then gave them 20 minutes to figure out how to improve it; they came up with 156 potential improvements to a product they considered perfect. Look for the overlooked and remember; everything can be improved.

Do you love your pet?
Would you be willing to pay just a little extra for products that stimulate your dog's mind? Judging by the success of Petstages, it turns out that, yes, you would.

←← Organising for new product development
➡ **Case study: Petstages**
↠ Smart plan: Part three

91

Smart plan: Part three

It's time to maximise the impact of the Smart Battery by choosing a name, creating a logo, creating packaging and figuring out what you want the brand to mean to consumers. By now you have studied the battery market, you've studied consumers' likes and dislikes in the battery category, you know quite a bit about your competition and you should be ready to create your own brand, name it, position it, package it and get some consumers' reactions to your creation.

If you were to write a product concept for the smart battery project described at the end of each chapter, it might look something like this:

Introducing the Smart Battery; the only battery that lasts ten times as long as a conventional alkaline battery.

Are you tired of batteries that don't work when you need them most? The problem is that regular alkaline batteries begin losing their power from the very time they are manufactured and only stop when they are dead.

Introducing the new Smart Battery; the first battery that actually shuts off when not in use. Unlike regular alkaline batteries, the Smart Battery has a computer chip that turns the battery off when it's not in use. Laboratory tests show the battery will last ten times as long as a normal alkaline battery so when you need the battery to be there for you, it will be.

Try the new Smart Battery – it lasts ten times as long.

Available wherever batteries are sold, priced at two for $7.50/£4.99/€5.99

What would you ask consumers about product concept? You might want to get reactions to the product benefit of lasting ten times as long. Is it believable? Do people know how long a regular alkaline battery lasts in the first place? Do they find it frustrating when barely used batteries don't work? Why do they think the barely used batteries don't work? How often do they experience this? Would it help if the battery was produced by a familiar name – such as Duracell? What about the computer chip; does this make sense to consumers? How much do they think a battery that lasts ten times as long as a normal battery should cost? Are there battery-run appliances, such as smoke alarms, that they would be more or less likely to use a Smart Battery in? Is Smart Battery a good name?

Smart Battery: Exercise three

Step 1) Develop a list of at least 25 different names for the Smart Battery. Determine which you believe are your three best names and write a concept statement for each, making all the statements exactly the same except the name. Show each statement to at least five people and ask their opinion of the name, its meaning, your logo, the colours you've chosen for the battery design and so on. From this determine the best name, battery design, logo design and colours.

Step 2) Write your positioning statement (something similar to the ones on pages 76–77). Determine where you want consumers to place your brand in their mind. Remember, keep the statement short and extremely focused (three to five words / one idea).

Chapter questions and exercises

1 Explain the differences between a product and a brand.
2 Name ten ways you could grow an existing brand such as Levi's jeans.
3 Define positioning in your own words and explain why it's important.
4 Name at least five brand contacts for your favourite product.
5 Develop the following:
   a) Five new chewing gum brands
   b) Five new cereal ideas
   c) Five new soft drinks
   d) A new shampoo different from any you've ever heard of.
6 Come up with one or two words that express the very essence of these brands: Nike, Apple, Starbucks, Gucci, Google, Nikon, eBay, Abercrombie.

Strategic pricing

Some Style Is Legendary

The Tiffany experience
If you could find a Tiffany watch for sale at your local jewellery store, would it really be a Tiffany watch? Yes and no. Of course, the Tiffany Company could manufacture it, but the Tiffany retail store is part of the entire Tiffany buying experience. That little blue box only comes from a real Tiffany store.

Tiffany & Co.

The next 'P' we'll be looking at is pricing. The price you charge your consumer can be too high (and therefore make an item either unaffordable or poor value) or too low (so you don't make enough profit or lead consumers to believe your product is poorly made). Like each of the other 'P's' in marketing, pricing is highly malleable and if used correctly can be a very strong strategic weapon. You can change pricing dramatically depending on what you are trying to accomplish. Getting pricing right is critical to your overall success in both the short and long term.

Chapter 4 will help you:

→ Discover how pricing can be a very potent strategic weapon.
→ See how profits can be increased both through raising revenues and cutting costs.
→ Learn that in the long run, value is more important than price.

Basics of marketing finance

Have you ever wondered what goes into the price of something you buy? The answer varies dramatically according to the way it's manufactured, distributed, promoted and sold. A container of milk travels from a cow, to a farmer, to a processing dairy, to a delivery service, to a retailer, to your home. The price you pay at the store covers all costs and provides profit to the farmer, the dairy, the delivery service and the retailer.

But it doesn't just have to cover the cost of the milk as a product. The price you pay has to help cover everything between the cow and your refrigerator. This covers things as mundane as packaging costs, lighting, shop workers, drivers and feed for the cows. You can imagine how this can become very complicated very quickly.

If you own a jewellers, you will probably make 85% of your sales and profits in the single month of December. In this case, you need to make adequate profits from each item you sell to cover your costs in months where sales will be very lean (such as August). The economics of different businesses are unique and can tell you quite a bit about what it takes to run them successfully.

What does it all mean?

The title of this section is 'Basics of marketing finance', and that's all we'll even be touching on here. For marketing students, future courses will expand dramatically on the basic concepts here to give you a solid understanding of marketing finance. First let's get used to some basic terminology:

→ **Sales:** the amount of product sold stated as either unit sales or in terms of currency.
→ **Costs:** the costs of manufacturing and selling products.
→ **Profit (or loss):** the difference between the total sales and total costs.
→ **Return on investment (ROI):** a ratio that shows the relative value of investing in one product vs. another.
→ **Retail price:** how much consumers pay to the retailer for the product they are buying.
→ **Retail mark-up:** the amount of money or percentage (then called a retail margin) the retailer adds to the price he pays to reach the retail price.
→ **Net price to retailer:** what the retailer pays the manufacturer for the product.
→ **Cost of goods:** How much it costs the manufacturer to produce the product.
→ **Direct expenses:** the costs for a manufacturer associated with selling the product (for example advertising and personal sales).
→ **Retailer margin:** the percentage of profit made when an item is sold. For example, if the retailer buys a widget for $1.00 and sells it for $2.00, their gross profit is $1.00 and gross margin is 50%.

96   **The Fundamentals of Marketing**

←← Product and brand development
→ **Strategic pricing**
→→ Distribution channel marketing

To put these terms into context, let's take a look at a bottle of shampoo; how much does the manufacturer actually profit from each bottle sold? Let's say the bottle sells for a retail price of US $5.00. The retailer purchased that bottle for $3.33 (net price to retailer) and marked it up by more than 40% (retail mark-up) to get to the retail price of $5.00.

What about costs and profits at the manufacturer? Remember, the manufacturer sold that same bottle of shampoo for $3.33. In this case, the cost of goods is roughly 60% of their sales price ($2.00), direct expenses to sell the bottle are about 25% of their sales price ($.83), leaving a profit of $.50 per bottle (15% profit margin).

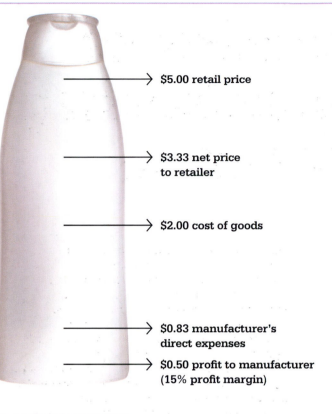

$5.00 retail price

$3.33 net price to retailer

$2.00 cost of goods

$0.83 manufacturer's direct expenses

$0.50 profit to manufacturer (15% profit margin)

Fig. 4-1: Typical cost structure
This is a fairly typical cost structure in the personal care industry. However, every business's percentages of mark-up and profit margins are different – depending on how much consumers are willing to pay for the particular item, how much competition there is and how different your brand truly is from its competitors.

Retailing and wholesaling

Generally speaking, the more hands a product has to pass through, the higher the price, as each of those people needs to cover costs plus profit. Conversely, of course, the fewer hands the items pass through, the lower the cost. Every product category we speak of is likely to have a different path from manufacturer to consumer.

Few manufacturers sell their products directly to consumers. When you buy fruit and vegetables at a farmers' market, you are buying directly from the manufacturer. However, when that same farmer sells goods to middlemen or grocery stores, additional steps are being built into the retail path and additional costs as well.

Manufacturers make goods and services. Wholesalers buy from manufacturers and turn around and sell to retail stores who then sell them to you the consumer. Larger manufacturers sell directly to large retailers and use wholesalers to sell to smaller stores.

For example, Procter & Gamble (P&G) is the sixth largest corporation in the world and one of the most successful marketers of health and beauty products, detergents and baby care products on the planet. P&G markets over 400 brands around the world with 24 brands having annual sales above $1 billion. When P&G sells to Wal-Mart (the largest retailer in the world), they sell directly. However, when P&G sells to small local stores around the world, they often use wholesalers who represent their products as well as the products of some of their competitors.

Most manufacturers have similar retail/wholesale systems. Fashion designer Ralph Lauren sells direct to consumers through his Polo stores, the Internet and outlet stores. He also sells through both high-end clothing stores and discount clothing stores. Sometimes these are different lines of clothing, sometimes they are the same product at radically different price points.

What factors determine pricing?

As you can imagine, the list of factors that determine how much you will charge for your product is nearly endless. We'll take a look at some of the major factors that need to be considered.

What is your objective?

Practised well, marketing is one of the most creative and disciplined forces on Earth. Nothing is haphazard, every decision is based on well thought-through objectives (what you want to accomplish) and strategies (how you will accomplish your objective).

There are two major marketing objectives: sales-driven objectives and profit-driven objectives. A sales-driven objective means that you want to maximise the units you sell. You may measure that by unit sales, dollar (currency) sales or market share. Brands often set sales objectives when they are relatively young or still in a growth phase. By maximising the total number of products sold, you are reaching the broadest possible audience and hoping to build loyalty to your brand. Profits may be secondary during this growth phase.

Profit-driven objectives aim to either maximise the overall profit the brand can deliver to the company or the profit per item. New products that begin with sales-driven objectives will frequently shift to a profit-driven objective once they have maximised their ongoing sales potential.

98   **The Fundamentals of Marketing**

← Product and brand development
→ **Strategic pricing**
→→ Distribution channel marketing

How flexible is your price?

Have you ever heard the term 'manufacturer's suggested retail price' or 'recommended retail price'? Often that is a nearly arbitrary price set only to establish a benchmark to which discounts can be applied. When you buy that bottle of shampoo we mentioned earlier, you will probably pay the full price the retailer tells you the item will cost you. Be assured that you are the only one to have paid a non-negotiated price. All prices are negotiated with hundreds of different types of discounting applied.

Manufacturers routinely offer quantity discounts to retailers. The more you buy, the less you pay per item. That allows you as a retailer to either make more money on every item you sell, or to pass the discount on to your consumers to make your shop more attractive than your competition.

Manufacturers offer temporary and seasonal price reductions; sometimes these are made just to help the manufacturer 'make their numbers' (sell all the units they had projected) or possibly to make their product more competitively priced during high-selling periods (beer in the summertime).

Manufacturers offer retailers discounts for paying their bills quickly (as well as penalties for paying slowly). Retailers charge manufacturers slotting fees, which are negotiated amounts of money for making shelf space available for new products (before the new product has proven its sales potential).

Consumers often get the benefit of negotiated prices in the form of consistently lower retail prices or through mechanisms that temporarily lower prices such as temporary price reductions, coupons, two-for-one deals or upsized products (when a manufacturer offers a bonus amount of product for the same price as the standard size) and so on.

How elastic is your price?

Price elasticity is a measurement of how much you can change your price without changing demand. For example, if you increase price by 10% and demand stays the same, your price is said to be elastic (you are still within an acceptable range for your consumer and demand remains unaffected). Should demand decrease significantly, your price is inelastic, meaning it cannot be changed without significant consequences. Obviously, elasticity is affected by supply of acceptable alternatives, economic conditions, your current price in the category compared to your competition and just about every other factor that affects price.

> **I have never known a concern to make a decided success that did not do good, honest work, and even in these days of fiercest competition, when everything would seem to be a matter of price, there lies still at the root of great business success the very much more important factor of quality.**
> Andrew Carnegie

What stage of the product life cycle are you in?

When a highly anticipated product comes to market, it's normal to price the item very high. Usually there is a group of innovators willing to pay almost anything to be among the first to own the item. This practice is called skim pricing because marketers are skimming off the top end of the target audience to get a very high price for a product before it becomes mainstream.

Skim pricing is often followed by penetration pricing, when the retail price is lowered to help the brand gain a greater penetration in the market. Remember Apple's introduction of the iPhone? In the US, the original $599 price tag was reduced to $399 within 66 days of its original introduction. While this is a normal product life cycle pricing strategy, in the case of the iPhone, Apple angered its innovators by dropping the price so dramatically and so quickly. Innovators are a critically important group to Apple's future success. Innovators start trends and Apple is a company that depends on trends. When Apple realised the level of dissatisfaction they had caused, they decided to give the innovators a $100 gift certificate to bring them back onside.

The iPhone example is common for highly anticipated products such as technology-driven items, video games or movies. But what about products consumers aren't clamouring for? They often apply exactly the opposite pricing strategy of introducing at a penetration price to encourage consumers to trial the product, and then raising the price once they have built enough market share and repeat business to sustain the brand. If McVitie's were to offer a new biscuit flavour, they might lower prices through coupons, in-store price reductions, even free samples, just to build up enough of a business base to sustain the new flavour.

How strong is demand?

Similar to the previous point, brands in high demand can charge far more than brands in low demand. When oil was selling for over $150 a barrel, the Toyota Prius was selling for up to $5,000 over the manufacturer's suggested retail price. That virtually never happens in the US, but with demand clearly outweighing supply, the cars were going to the highest bidder. At the same time, Toyota could barely give away the Toyota Sequoia, their largest, most gas-guzzling SUV. When demand is strong, you can price accordingly. When demand falls, often the prices consumers are willing to pay drop as well.

When Nintendo introduced the Wii game system just prior to Christmas 2006, demand was so high the product was selling on auction websites such as eBay for up to double its full retail price. As supply met demand, prices decreased to the point where you could buy the product at a discount within a year.

100   **The Fundamentals of Marketing**

←← Product and brand development
→ **Strategic pricing**
→→ Distribution channel marketing

Geographic pricing

While in the US it is illegal to sell the same item to one person at one price while you sell it to another at another price (Robinson-Patman Act of 1936), there are often geographic differences brought on in part by the variance in things such as transportation costs and real estate costs. A cup of coffee at Starbucks will cost you more in a big city like Paris than in a small provincial town. And it will cost you even more in an airport… because, everything does.

How long is your mark-up chain?

As mentioned earlier, the closer you are to the source/manufacturer, the fewer mark-ups you'll need to build in to your price. Keep in mind, however, that even in the very simple example we gave earlier of a farmer selling directly to you at a farmers' market, there are mark-ups hidden in the cost of seeds, fertiliser and all the machinery the farmer needs. All of these affect what the farmer has to charge in order to make a profit and ultimately those costs all get passed along to the consumer.

How fast is turnover?

Turnover refers to how often you turn over (sell) your total inventory. Bread is purchased on a regular basis by the majority of the world's population and therefore has a very fast turnover. It's baked, stocked and sold within a short period of time. Jewellery, on the other hand, has a very slow turnover. A retailer might stock a necklace that sits in the store for 12–18 months before just the right buyer comes along. Faster turnover allows for lower prices and profit margins because sales are reasonably regular. Slower turnover items may require much higher prices and higher profit margins to cover their infrequent purchase timing.

Speculation is only a word covering the making of money out of the manipulation of prices, instead of supplying goods and services.
Henry Ford

Profit – the bottom line

While marketers have many roles, ultimately their role is to drive the profitability of a company. Profit is the money you have left over from sales after taking out all costs and taxes. Most companies are owned by the stock-owning public. When people buy stock it is because they expect the value of the stock to increase and therefore make them more money. Stock grows as the value of the company grows, which occurs as a result of sales increases and even more importantly, profit growth.

Maximising profitability

Marketers are constantly struggling to find the maximum profitability for their brands. The price determines the quantity you will sell and the quantity you make determines your price per item (generally your price per item decreases as the quantity increases). Maximum profitability is found where the marginal revenue from each item sold is equal to, or greater than, the marginal cost of that item. In simpler terms, profit increases as long as you can make more revenue from selling an additional item than it costs to make it. While that sounds simple, in a competitive market maximising sales and price can be very difficult to achieve. Competitors are forcing you to lower your prices as they attempt to push your sales down.

Most brands never reach their maximum profitability, or if they do it is a very temporary event in a constantly evolving marketplace. So how can we increase profits? There are two basic ways to increase profitability: increase prices and/or cut costs.

Driving profits through price increases

Increasing prices when costs and sales remain steady will increase profitability at least in the short term. Longer term, price increases tend to inspire your suppliers to increase their prices as well, causing your costs to increase. Equally, raising your prices can lead to declining sales as your competitors step in to take advantage of their pricing advantages. In very low profit margin businesses such as airlines, competitors will often follow the leader in either increasing or decreasing prices in order to minimise price as a brand selection determinant.

102   **The Fundamentals of Marketing**

←← Product and brand development
→ **Strategic pricing**
→→ Distribution channel marketing

Driving profitability through cutting costs

Cutting costs can be an even more effective way of increasing profitability. You'll recall from Chapter 1 that the 1980s was the era of the low-cost producer. Manufacturers, led by their finance departments, looked for inefficiencies throughout the manufacturing, shipping and storage systems. They looked for ways to decrease manufacturing costs, which led to manufacturing being moved from North America and Europe into China, India and any country with relatively low manufacturing costs. Companies relocated not just manufacturing but customer service to places such as Bangalore, India, where the population is highly educated, but costs are still dramatically below world averages.

There are thousands of ways to lower costs. Manufacturers in North America and Europe have recently been downsizing packaging, thereby selling less product for the same or higher prices. How many grammes of Kellogg's Corn Flakes are in a box? I don't know and chances are you don't either. If Kellogg's decides to lower the amount they sell us by 10g, chances are no one would notice (especially if they leave it in the same size box). Eventually, they could introduce new smaller or thinner packaging and again we probably wouldn't notice.

Is this preoccupation with lowering costs good for us as consumers? Not always, but we all do like paying as little as possible for products. So, our drugs are made in India and China along with most of our electronics, clothing and even now our food.

Manufacturers' cost-cutting tactics

Cheaper ingredients	Decreased warranties	Decreased shipping costs	Relocate support staff (such as accounting customer service) offshore
Off-shore manufacturing	Automated manufacturing	Poorer-quality goods	Radically changing format of product such as CD to downloadable music sales
Cheaper packaging	Ingredients removed or replaced	Passing along costs to consumer (such as shipping)	Selling direct to consumers
Less product per package	More efficient / less expensive sales force	Becoming more local	Lower staff salaries and benefits

←← Basics of marketing finance
→ **Profit – the bottom line**
→→ Pricing strategies

103

Globalisation, profit growth and strategy

Why sell to 62 million UK citizens or US 306 million citizens of the US if you can sell to more than six billion citizens of the world? Companies first looked for new markets to sell their products in, and then new markets to manufacture their products in; globalisation of brands and marketing has now fundamentally changed the world.

In many ways this move has helped many struggling countries and spread wealth once concentrated in a few markets a bit more evenly. China, India and Brazil now have some of the healthiest economies in the world and opportunities abound like never before. The long-term effect will be a redistribution of wealth, flattening the world into (more or less) a single economy. For companies, this globalisation has helped soften the highs and lows a single country's economy might experience. If business is weak in the US, chances are it's stronger in Asia and continuing to grow globally.

Eventually the cost of doing business will (theoretically) more or less even out around the world, lessening competitive advantages of one country over another and disparities of standard of living. When that occurs, jobs will probably relocate simply to the most efficient markets.

Globalisation's impact on corporate value

The job of a public company is to increase the value of the corporation. Corporate value is measured through the value of its stock and everything a company does must in the long term help grow the value of the corporation. Globalisation has had a major impact on the value of many corporations as it has allowed them to increase manufacturing efficiency, sell to a larger audience and realise cost savings in growing global brands.

104   **The Fundamentals of Marketing**

⟵ Product and brand development
→ **Strategic pricing**
⟶ Distribution channel marketing

Creating value in a low price world

Target and K-Mart are two US-based discount department stores that compete directly with Wal-Mart. As Wal-Mart grew in size and dominance, both K-Mart and Target were caught in a no-win situation. Neither could match Wal-Mart's low prices with Wal-Mart at one time buying up literally 30% of China's exports.

K-Mart continued to try and match Wal-Mart prices. However, with older run-down stores often in deteriorating sections of town and Wal-Mart's superior distribution systems, K-Mart couldn't win. K-Mart sold its stores in 2004.

Target followed a different route. Target stores concentrated on creating customer value. Wal-Mart prices might be lower, but Target's overall shopping experience was vastly superior. Target told consumers in their advertising and on the front of their stores to 'expect more' – clearly a dig at Wal-Mart. If Wal-Mart is a discount store, Target referred to itself as a discount department store. The stores were cleaner and brighter, the aisles were wider, the merchandise was generally higher quality and Target got prominent fashion and industrial designers to create special lines of everything from clothing to toasters, all sold exclusively through Target stores (as with this Sonia Kashuk make-up, shown above).

The shopping experience inside a Wal-Mart store can be loud, confusing and stressful. But the prices are low. Target, on the other hand, delivers a shopping experience where customers are delighted and surprised to have found relatively low prices in such a nice store.

This isn't to say that Target has a better idea than Wal-Mart. Wal-Mart built a $379 billion revenue business by focusing on delivering the lowest possible prices. Target is a distant #2 retailer at $64 billion, but that's not the point. The point is that Target is alive and well when so many others drowned in Wal-Mart's wake. And, if you look around, you'll see Wal-Mart stores becoming cleaner, newer and nicer with designer label merchandise – like Target.

←← Basics of marketing finance
→ **Profit – the bottom line**
→→ Pricing strategies

105

Pricing strategies

By now you've seen that pricing is more involved than figuring out how much the item costs you to manufacture and simply adding a profit margin to it. Marketers use pricing as a competitive weapon against their rivals just as they do with each of the other 'P's'. Let's take a look at the strategic side of pricing.

You can make more money by making more products and charging higher prices. You can make more money by making more products and charging lower prices. And, you can make more money by making more products and charging both higher and lower prices.

In Chapter 1 we saw that Godiva are somewhat selective in their distribution, they make a lot of chocolate and at the prices they sell it for, annual sales top $500 million. However, if Godiva becomes too widely distributed they will no longer be able to charge such a high price.

You can make more money by selling for lower prices. Wal-Mart became the world's largest retailer focusing on low prices. Does everything in a Wal-Mart store actually cost less than anywhere else? No. But enough of the items you buy on a regular basis do, which enables Wal-Mart to hold on to that reputation.

In the grocery business, consumers know the prices of about a dozen items in a shop. If you price your bread at double the market average then you can bet that first, your customers will notice and secondly, they will assume everything in your shop is ridiculously overpriced. The same is true for most everyday products such as milk, butter, eggs and meat. However, how much should we pay for a can of tomatoes? If a shop prices them 10% higher than their competitors it's likely that most customers will never notice. This is true for 99% of the items in a shop. If you price low on the items people know, you can probably get away with charging a little more on the others.

You can make more money by selling more product for higher and lower prices. Ralph Lauren does this better than just about anyone and has always been brilliant at pricing their goods. The flagship Polo store at 72nd and Madison Avenue in New York City can charge nearly $500 for a man's dress shirt. The discount clothing store TJ Maxx (known as TK Maxx in the UK and Europe), also sells Ralph Lauren Polo dress shirts, for about $20.00 each. Lauren has designed about 40 different lines of clothing at different price points and different exclusivity levels keeping the brand as one of the most respected in the world, but also making it the largest clothing manufacturer in America.

Cost plus pricing

The basic tenet of all pricing strategies is cost plus pricing. You simply figure out how much it costs you to manufacturer the item, add your marketing costs and profit and there you have your price. This is a good starting point, but marketers need to be aware of more than just their costs. If your competition is making a good product and it costs half as much, clearly this simple model has let you down.

106   **The Fundamentals of Marketing**

⇐ Product and brand development
➜ **Strategic pricing**
⇒ Distribution channel marketing

Expectation pricing

Consumers tend to have a pretty decent idea of how much things should cost. For this reason, if you look at an entire category of goods you'll generally find that the prices of the various brands don't vary by more than 10%.

That said, however, expectation pricing doesn't always work. When VW introduced the Phaeton luxury car into the US market in 2004 they priced it at luxury car levels (between $68,000 and $100,000). As a result, they sold only 1,433 the first year, just over 800 the second year and pulled the car off the market midway through the third year. Their pricing was certainly at the correct luxury-expectation level, so why didn't it work? The problem was that VW is a very well-established brand, a well-respected brand and even a well-loved brand. But it's not a luxury brand. The word Volkswagen is German for 'people's car' and the people's car doesn't cost $100,000. VW has announced it will reintroduce the Phaeton, but until they meet the expectations they have spent millions setting, they can't expect pricing alone to make it a luxury car.

Competitive alignment pricing

When you price according to competitors' prices (not necessarily what consumers expect), it is called competitive alignment pricing. Most product categories have reasonably similar prices among all the competitors.

Loss-leader pricing

A loss-leader is an item that a retailer is willing to lose money on in order to increase foot traffic in their shop. For example, when you see Pampers on sale at very low prices, you know the retailer is trying to encourage young families to shop at the store and is willing to lose money on the purchase of Pampers because they believe they will make up that loss and make a respectable profit on the entire shopping visit. Typical loss-leaders include milk, orange juice, butter, beer and razors (once a consumer likes the handle, they'll keep buying the blades).

Bait and switch pricing

'Bait and switch' describes the questionable practice of advertising a particular product at a very low price, and then when the customer arrives at the store sales people try to persuade them to make a different (more expensive) purchase. It's certainly unethical and in the US it's illegal. But since it is nearly impossible to effectively regulate, it is a fairly common practice especially among car dealers that advertise one particular car at a price just to increase foot traffic among people who probably won't have the opportunity to even see the car.

Retailers considering a competitive pricing strategy will need to provide outstanding customer service to stand above the competition.
Shari Waters

← Profit – the bottom line
→ **Pricing strategies**
→→ Case study: Exotic water

107

Prestige pricing

Pricing communicates. What's the difference between a relatively cheap bottle of sparkling wine from California that you or I might buy at the local supermarket and an extremely expensive bottle of Cristal champagne? The answer is expectations. You expect a glass of Cristal to be otherworldly and for a few it is. By setting an eye-watering price per bottle, you have communicated that this is the very best champagne available and even better than Dom Pérignon, which sells for around a third of the price.

Prestige pricing is not just limited to prestige products such as champagne. When Dyson introduced a vacuum cleaner priced at almost twice the average of its competitors in the product category, they redefined what people would be willing to pay if they thought the vacuum was actually better quality. The same is true of Starbucks, particularly in the US. Before Starbucks, coffee was an absolute commodity selling at cost prices. Starbucks made us appreciate coffee again and we are willing to pay high prices for the privilege.

Bid pricing

How much is item 'X' worth? Quite simply, it is worth as much as someone is willing to pay for it. Bid pricing gets you to exactly what people are willing to pay for an item. Auction websites such as eBay sell just about anything and allow customers to determine a product's worth. The price for a product that is in high demand and low supply is likely to go substantially over the manufacturer's recommended retail price.

For example, front row seats to a U2 concert might sell for a relatively reasonable price at the box office. However, if the show is sold out, or it's during a holiday weekend, or their latest album has just won some major awards, then that seat may be worth five times the original box office value. Auction websites (where legal) allow you to get the full value of the item as determined by the buyer.

Bundle pricing

It's in a marketer's self-interest to sell you as much as possible. So some marketers will bundle multiple products together to encourage you to buy more of their offerings. For example, Time-Warner is primarily a cable provider but they also sell home security, Internet telephone, pay-per-view movies as well as magazines and movies. By signing up for cable TV, phone and home security, consumers are given a bundle price that is the equivalent of getting the home security for free.

Competitive pricing advantages

To use pricing as a competitive advantage you may need to lower your price – or you may need to raise it. Price signals better quality, exclusivity and raises expectations. Would Starbucks have become so popular with low or average prices? Absolutely not. The high price in part signalled specialness to people and got them to try it at least once. If the brand delivered, and it did, then the very fundamentals of what coffee is and who consumes it changed forever.

In the US there is a direct marketing company called Omaha Steaks <www.omahasteaks.com>. They sell steaks through the mail for seven times the price typically

⭠ Product and brand development
➜ **Strategic pricing**
⇢ Distribution channel marketing

charged by a local butcher. Twenty-five adults were asked to rate Omaha Steaks against their local butcher's equivalent cut. None of the respondents had ever tasted an Omaha Steak. They only viewed the website complete with prices. All but one said that they thought the Omaha Steak would taste 'substantially better' than their local butcher's steak. Their reasons ranged from Omaha being a 'cattle town' to 'healthier cows' to 'better butchers'.

The communicative power of price is enormous; in this case it led nearly everyone asked to say that they would rather have a steak sent through the mail from approximately 2,000 miles away rather than one freshly butchered less than two miles away. It defies logic, but gives you an idea of what a powerful communicator price can be.

Legal and ethical constraints on pricing

Laws vary dramatically country by country and even within a country. There are states in the US where it is illegal to sell a product below its cost (in an effort to protect smaller retailers that may not be able to compete under such circumstances). Most areas of the world have some laws or accepted practices meant to create a fair selling environment.

In the US, the Robinson-Patman Act of 1936 makes price discrimination illegal (in other words, I sell the same item to you at one price and to someone else at a different price. The Wheeler Lea Amendment bans 'unfair or deceptive acts in commerce'. An example of this would include the use of spurious list prices. If I tell you the price of a car is $30,000, but I will sell it to you for $10,000, you might feel like you got an amazing deal. But what if you found out that the list price of the car was always $10,000?

Price fixing is illegal in most countries. When competitive manufacturers get together and agree on how much they will charge for a particular product that is known as price fixing. For example, in 2009 the Japan Fair Trade Commission fined electronics firm Sharp 261.07 million yen ($3 million) for suspected price-fixing with Hitachi of liquid-crystal displays. In 2008, the leading chocolate makers in the world were accused of price fixing around the Valentine's Day holiday when chocolate sales are at their peak.

Slotting fees are also considered unethical by many; these are the fees retailers charge marketers to get shelf space for new products. These can easily go into the tens of millions of dollars for large chain stores dealing with large manufacturers. What is unethical about this? After all, the shelf space is worth quite a bit to both the retailer and the manufacturer. The problem is slotting fees can exclude smaller companies that can't afford them. While that may not seem like a problem in the short term, longer term it means everything we get only comes from a few large companies, and that's not something any of us wants.

As we've just seen, the most common legal issue in pricing is bait and switch pricing where a retailer advertises a product at an absurdly low price and then sales people switch consumers to more expensive items. Although illegal, retailers routinely get around the law by having limited quantities (which can be as few as one) of the advertised item. By the time you've gone to the store, that item is sold and sales people concentrate on selling you higher-priced substitutes.

← Profit – the bottom line
→ **Pricing strategies**
→→ Case study: Exotic water

109

Creating customer value

While pricing is important, it is only a means to an end. The more important concept is customer value. If consumers feel they have received an excellent product for their money, you have created customer value.

All of us have been to restaurants that promised great food and charged a lot of money but at the end left us feeling we hadn't received our money's worth. How do we react? We simply don't return and we may advise our friends and family not to go.

But what is value and how do we create it? Value is the belief that expectations have been met or exceeded for the money we have spent. Because it is an individual assessment, no two people measure value in exactly same way.

We create value by delivering more than the consumer expects. For example, the product quality may be better than expected, the product may last longer than expected, delivery may occur more quickly than expected and so

on. The general rule in business is to under-promise and over-deliver. This is not just the case in the business world; consider politics. The first thing a newly elected politician does is attempt to lower expectations both in terms of what will get accomplished and how quickly it will get accomplished. Similarly, if you tell me you can sell ten widgets and you sell ten widgets, you have given me what you promised and nothing more. If you tell me you are going to sell eight widgets and sell those same ten, you are a hero.

Starbucks creates value by having clean and comfortable restaurants, relaxing music, the freshest coffee possible and speciality coffee drinks customers can't get anywhere else. McDonald's creates value by keeping prices low, stores clean and food fresh and hot. Hyundai creates value by giving warranties on their cars that are two or three times as long as other manufacturers. Even some rock stars understand the concept of value by playing three-hour concerts so that the audience feel they have received even more than they have paid for.

What we obtain too cheap we esteem too little; it is dearness only that gives everything value.
Thomas Paine

110   **The Fundamentals of Marketing**

←← Product and brand development
→ **Strategic pricing**
→→ Distribution channel marketing

A strong brand can sell for a little and a lot and still be a strong brand... Nike

If you are ever in New York City, wander over to the corner of 57th Street and 5th Avenue. Besides being some of the most expensive retail real estate in the world, it's the home of Niketown, one of Nike's 12 flagship stores selling all their newest shoes, clothing and equipment. A pair of Nike basketball shoes can sell for $300, and if they are a limited edition, they will fetch up to ten times that at auction once they are sold out. When you leave New York, you'll see many different off-price discounters such as TJ Maxx, Marshalls, Famous Footwear and more. There you can probably pick up a pair of basketball shoes for about $30 and clothing starting at less than $10.

How can a company sell products through exclusive flagship stores and discount stores and not hurt their brand?

The truth is that not many brands could pull this off. Nike is a brand with a very clear meaning to its consumers. Nike is all about performing at your personal best, not quality or fashion or style. When your brand has a clear meaning to its consumers that has been communicated consistently for so many years, discount stores can't cheapen the brand. Rather than selling discount product, anything with the Nike logo on it is Nike that just happens to cost less than in the flagship stores.

Now contrast the strength of Nike with some weaker brands such as K-Swiss, Fila and Champion, which have become second-rate discount brands in large part by selling at discount stores.

←← Profit – the bottom line
→ **Pricing strategies**
→→ Case study: Exotic water

111

Case study: Exotic water

We don't market products. We market brands. We do this for the simple reason that brands, with all the added value we can bring to these mere products, are worth more money than products are. Let's see how the world's second most plentiful resource, water, was turned from a common commodity people expect for free to a relatively expensive and exotic brand.

Bling H$_2$O
Bling H$_2$O is bottled at source in Dandridge, Tennessee, using a nine-step purification process that includes ozone, ultraviolet and micro-filtration.

A world of choice
There are more than 80 different brands of bottled water available for sale in the US today with more being introduced every day. They all contain basically the same thing – water. Why do we need more than 80 different brands of water? Of course, we don't. However, where there is a new positioning idea, there can be a new brand idea, which in turn may inspire consumers to pay even more… for something that comes out of the kitchen tap for free.

Here is a sample of how positioning can take a commodity like water and make it worth more and more money to some consumers.

Aquafina: The number one water brand in the US bottled by PepsiCo, selling for $.06 per ounce.

Fiji Water: Water imported from Fiji and supposedly President Obama's favourite, sells for $.10 per ounce.

Ethos Water: Bottled by PepsiCo, Ethos donates a small portion of the sale towards securing clean water for developing countries. Ethos sells for $.11 per ounce.

Tasmanian Rain: Australian water selling for $.11 per ounce.

Tau: Sparkling water from Wales selling for $.12 per ounce.

Bling H$_2$O: Created by a Hollywood screenwriter and selling for $1.13 per ounce.

Bling H$_2$O comes in limited edition, corked reusable frosted glass bottles – complete with handcrafted Swarovski crystals. It is the inspiration of Kevin G. Boyd, Hollywood writer-producer. While working on various studio lots where image is of the utmost importance he noticed that you could tell a lot about a person by the bottled water they carried.

←← Product and brand development
➜ **Strategic pricing**
⟶ Distribution channel marketing

According to Boyd, in Hollywood it seemed as if people flaunted their bottled water like it was part of their presentation. He therefore made it Bling H$_2$O's mission to 'offer a product with an exquisite face to match exquisite taste. The product is strategically positioned to target the expanding super-luxury consumer market. Initially introduced to hand-selected athletes and actors, Bling H$_2$O is now excitedly expanding its availability. Bling H$_2$O is pop culture in a bottle. But it's not for everyone, just those that Bling.'

Straight from the tap
If Bling isn't for you, how about TAP'D NY. This is unapologetic tap water from New York City that is sold through coffee shops for $1.50 with ads that say 'refillable at any New York City tap'. That's right, the same water that flows out of taps all over New York City for free has been bottled by Craig Zucker who designed a logo and is selling tap water. Is he successful? It's working so well that he's currently expanding the idea to other cities.

One of the world's best new advertising agencies, droga5, even managed to figure out how to get Americans to pay $1.00 a glass for straight tap water in restaurants. UNICEF asked for their help in raising awareness and funds to get safe drinking water to children around the world. According to UNICEF 4,200 children die every year from water-borne diseases and 900 million people don't have regular access to safe drinking water. It's the 21st century and we haven't figured out something this basic for 15% of the world's population. UNICEF and droga5 worked out that by asking New York restaurant patrons to pay $1 for their tap water, they could begin to help.

The project began in 2007 with 300 restaurants in New York City. Today, thousands of restaurants across the US participate and the programme is likely to expand next into Europe and beyond. Who would have guessed that a very simple idea about the world's second largest commodity could change the lives of so many?

Moral of the story
Anything can be branded, with value added to make it worth more money. It is likely that clean and drinkable water is available to those of you reading this book. I have a water fountain right down the hall from where I am typing this that will give me all the cold, pure water I could ever want. So why would I pay for the world's second largest commodity when I can get it free? People will pay for anything if you can add value to it. For the designer waters there is the experience of tasting water from faraway lands, or often more importantly, being seen with a more exotic water than your friends. That's right: water can be a status symbol, and then how much is it worth? Clearly Fiji Water must be more exotic than Evian since it comes from even further away and because Fiji is a more exotic location than France. Make sense? If you said no, congratulations, you aren't falling for marketing. If you said yes, I'd like to sell you a bottle of water from the South Pole – that's even further away and more exotic. Or, we could just raise money and awareness with tap water and do some good.

If we can make water into a branded value-added product (and we have, many times over), we can turn anything into a branded product (check out the oxygen bars that started in Japan and are all over the world now – that's right, people are paying for oxygen).

← Pricing strategies
→ **Case study: Exotic water**
⇾ Smart plan: Part four

113

Smart plan: Part four

So, how much should you charge for a battery with a brain? Batteries are a commodity in most countries, with few successful brands, and always a price leader that keeps the category prices low. It's certainly possible to charge too much and drive customers away. You could also charge too little and either not cover your costs or make too small a profit to make the venture worth doing. So, how do you figure it out?

Smart Battery: Exercise four

Step one: How much does the competition charge? In order to determine a price for our battery we have to do some research into how much comparable batteries cost in discount stores, corner shops and supermarkets . To keep this project simple, let's focus only on battery size AA.

You are right in thinking that there are no directly comparable batteries on the market, but consumers are using brands now that we hope to replace with our new battery. We'll use that.

Step two: What will consumers be willing to pay for a battery that lasts ten times as long as their conventional alkaline battery? Ask ten adults familiar with buying batteries by exposing them to the concept statement and asking open-ended questions to discover their expected price.

Step three: Set your pricing objective. As this is a new product, you will probably want a sales-driven strategy to build substantial market share before you worry too much about reaping large profits.

114 The Fundamentals of Marketing

⇐ Product and brand development
➡ **Strategic pricing**
⇉ Distribution channel marketing

Step four: Determine your pricing strategy from the different strategies mentioned earlier in the chapter. Many of you are likely to be interested in the prestige pricing strategy. Just remember that only the battery purchaser knows what kind of battery is being used; they are invisible and therefore void of any sort of prestige.

Step five: Propose a wholesale and retail price for a package of four batteries that will cover all costs at whatever profit level you deem reasonable. For the sake of this exercise, assume that the manufacturing and marketing cost is $1.50 per battery.

Chapter questions and exercises

Category pricing behaviour

1 Visit a supermarket and compare the prices on competitive brands in a single product category (for example, ground coffee, aspirin, colas, yogurts or peanut butter). What do you think the different brands are trying to communicate to consumers via the differing prices?

Price flexibility

2 Make a list of all the different types of discounts you can find in a grocery store (for example, frequent buyer clubs and coupons).

Types of pricing

3 Take a single product most people are familiar with buying, such as a DVD. Ask 20 adults how much they are willing to pay for a new DVD to measure their expectation price. Average the responses. How does that number compare with major retail outlets and online stores?

Bait and switch pricing

4 Find an example of bait and switch pricing in your local newspaper or online. How are they getting around the laws to remain legal?

Distribution channel marketing

Have you ever seen an Avon store?
Don't worry. No one has. Avon doesn't have shops. Avon has used door-to-door sales representatives to sell their goods since 1886. Today they have nearly five million men and women selling door to door in over 100 countries. That's like having five million stores.

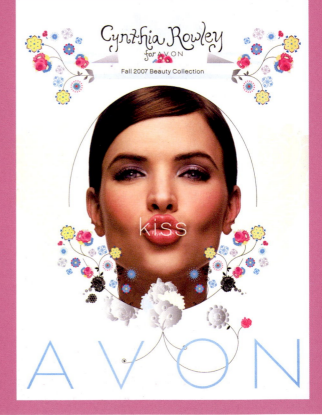

Our penultimate 'P' is 'place – also known as 'distribution'. Need a diamond ring? You could get one from an exclusive designer jewellery shop, or you could get it from the QVC shopping channel. Is the designer ring better than the QVC ring? Not necessarily. Is the designer diamond ring more expensive than the QVC ring? Absolutely! Will your memory of getting a designer ring be different to your memory of getting a QVC diamond ring? More than likely. Where you sell and where you buy can have a huge impact on your quantity of sales and your profitability per item.

Chapter 5 will help you:

➜ **Maximise sales and/or profits through channel marketing.**
➜ **Learn about different distribution strategies and how to determine which is best for you.**
➜ **Design and manage your channel strategy.**
➜ **Discover customer relationship marketing (CRM).**

What are distribution channels and how do they work?

The term channel is used to describe the trip a product takes from the manufacturer all the way to the end-user. There may be multiple destinations on this trip or just a single destination, but in either case, it is a trip through a channel.

One thing we should point out at the beginning of the chapter is that ultimately this is all about making as much money as you can. And, it's all about the money at every level of the distribution channel. The manufacturer wants to make as much as possible, the middlemen want to make as much as possible, the retailer wants to make as much as possible and the consumer wants to pay as little as possible. Further, being all about the money can determine how much you charge the next in line or how much your costs are and what costs can be pushed off your plate onto someone else's. If that seems harsh, it will all make more sense as you realise just how many steps there are between the manufacturer and the end-user.

Most retailers made major mistakes of putting their distribution centres at greater distances from each other when energy prices came down and stayed stable in the 80s and 90s . Retailers are long-hauling freight anywhere from 300 to 700 miles. With 50 cents a mile for a 20-ton diesel freight truck, it adds up.

Burt Flickinger

118   The Fundamentals of Marketing

← Strategic pricing
→ **Distribution channel marketing**
→→ Promotion in marketing

Some basic definitions

Before we get too far along, let's take a look at some of the terminology we are about to start using.

Manufacturer/marketer

The manufacturer is the person or company that actually makes whatever product you are trying to sell. The term marketer is used interchangeably, but sometimes is a different person or company. Marketer refers more accurately to the person or company that creates product, sets pricing, determines how and where to sell the product, determines to whom the product should be sold and promotes the product to its intended audience. Obviously there is much more to marketing a product than there is to simply manufacturing a product.

Channel of distribution (COD)

This refers to the journey a product takes from manufacturer to end-user including whatever retailers or wholesalers are between the manufacturer and end-user. This term is often used just to refer to retailers alone, but more accurately refers to the full journey.

End-user

The end-user is the actual user of the product. In many instances the person who buys a product is different from the end-user. For example, men's underwear is mostly purchased by women for the men in their life. Marketers must find ways to attract both buyers and users when they are different.

Retailer

A retailer is the person or company that sells goods to those that buy or use the product.

Wholesaler or broker

This refers to someone between the manufacturer and the retailer that buys from the manufacturer and sells to the retailer.

Direct marketing, Internet marketing, and catalogue marketing

The main ways employed to sell products directly from the manufacturer or wholesalers to purchasers/end-users.

Sales force

A sales force is the team of people representing either the manufacturer or some middleman and selling to either retailers or sometimes directly to the consumer/end-user (such as Avon).

Independent sales representative or agent

Manufacturers often handle the larger retailers with their own sales force. However, they will also sell their wares to independent sales representatives that sell directly to retailers too small or numerous to be handled efficiently by the manufacturer.

Direct channels of distribution and indirect channels of distribution

There are two basic types of channel: direct and indirect. A direct channel means the manufacturer makes and sells the item to the end-user. While this may seem like a very common approach, it's actually fairly unusual. Procter & Gamble and Unilever are two of the largest manufacturers in the world, but you don't see them selling what they make in P&G or Unilever stores (and the few times they have tried have been miserable failures). However, direct channels are growing again for the first time in decades. The Apple Store, Niketown, the Sony Store and Avon are all examples of a direct channel of distribution as are the outlet shops that are growing in popularity in the fashion world.

There are many reasons you might want to control distribution through direct channels. The first is that you have control over the entire retail experience. You design the stores, you determine where they should be located, no one ever has a sale that cheapens your product, you make it, you sell it, you service it and you control the relationship with the end-user. You also don't have to share the profits with anyone else, but don't forget those stores all cost a tremendous amount of money that you are responsible for now.

Using an indirect channel of distribution means that you sell your product to someone else who sells to the end-user. Indirect channels of distribution make up about 95% of all consumer-marketing.

Indirect channels of distribution are the choice of most manufacturers because they are the choice of most consumers. Consumers love one-stop shopping and indirect channels allow for competing products to sit side-by-side on a shelf and compete for consumers. Indirect channels also allow customers to get service locally, give your brand a local presence in every size of community and are just simpler for manufacturers than trying to set up shops everywhere.

There are some disadvantages as well. When you turn your product over to a third party, you lose control of how it is presented to your end-user. Compare how an iPod is presented in an Apple Store with how it is presented in large electronics discounters. You'll see that although Apple is trying desperately, the retail experience in an Apple Store and a discount shop simply can't be equal. The same is true for pricing. Once you sell to a third party, you lose some control over how much is charged for your product. Remember, charging too little could hurt your long-term reputation and actually damage the brand.

Mixed distribution channels

Most manufacturers employ very complicated distribution channels that mix both direct (from manufacturer to consumer) and indirect (manufacturer to various middlemen including retailers) channels of distribution. As marketing manager, your job is to grow the sales of your product however you can. Sometimes that comes from consumers buying more, and sometimes it comes from finding new markets to sell to. Managing your channels of distribution will allow you to do this, and as Figure 5-1 shows there are many options to choose from.

120   **The Fundamentals of Marketing**

⬅⬅ Strategic pricing
➡ **Distribution channel marketing**
➡➤ Promotion in marketing

Fig. 5-1: Distribution channels
The range of distribution channels
available to marketing managers.

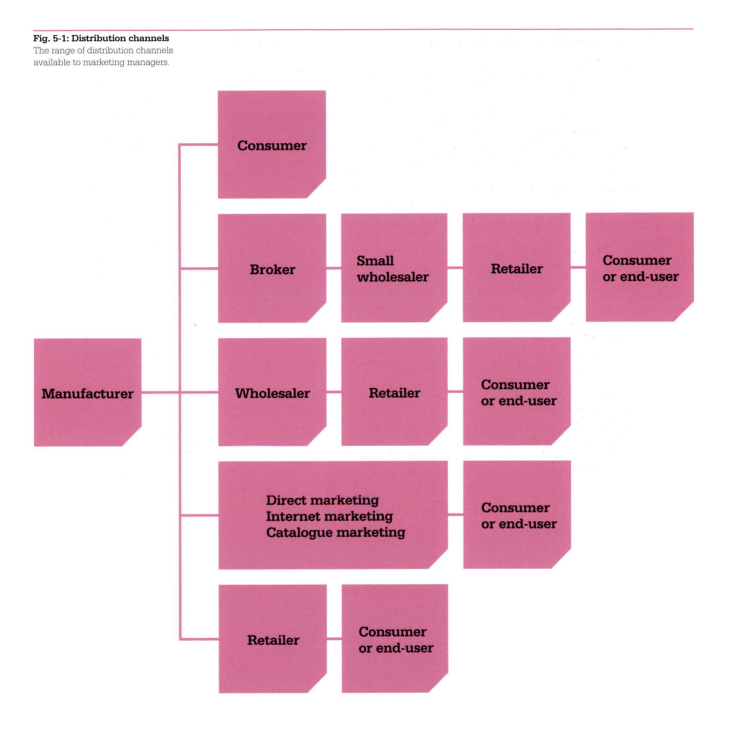

Distribution strategies

In Chapter 1 (pages 16–17) we discussed that Godiva chocolates are available only in Godiva stores, online and in select department stores. Godiva consciously choose to make the product somewhat difficult to find. Generally products that are available everywhere become very commonplace and Godiva needs to remain a special purchase in order to get the high prices they are charging. Mars, on the other hand, wants to be seen as an everyday treat that is available everywhere. These are two opposite distribution strategies, but both are right for their particular product.

Which strategy?

Before the first product is sold the marketing manager must determine which distribution strategy they want to follow. There are three basic strategies. Each is different and each is the right strategy for some brands and the wrong strategy for other brands. They are:
1) Be ubiquitous
2) Selective distribution
3) Exclusive distribution

Be ubiquitous

This strategy requires you to employ as wide a distribution system as possible. Coca-Cola talks about being available within an arm's length of desire. Wherever in the world you might be reading this, if I sent you out to get a Coca-Cola or Pepsi-Cola, with only a few exceptions, you could probably bring one back within five minutes. Coke and Pepsi want to be everywhere, they want to be commonplace and they want to be thought of as an everyday beverage. No matter what product category you are talking about you can find some brand that wants to be easily accessible and available at arm's length. McDonald's, Pantene shampoo, Jaffa Cakes in Europe are all trying to be ubiquitous.

Selective distribution

Selective distribution is the process of carefully selecting where you want to be available and where you do not want to be available. Godiva chocolates are a good example of selective distribution. The Godiva shops are beautiful chocolate emporiums where the product is handled like fine jewels and sold one at a time. They also sell online (available to anyone with a computer and credit card, but still maintaining more credibility that any mass retailer). Finally, Godiva is for sale at fine department stores (such as Macy's/Bloomingdale's in the US and Harrods in the UK, or KDF in Berlin). You won't find Godiva in discount shops (except, ironically, their coffees). Godiva remains somewhat exclusive by not selling everywhere. In doing so, they may be limiting their total sales potential, but are keeping the product worthy of its high price.

122   **The Fundamentals of Marketing**

←← Strategic pricing
→ **Distribution channel marketing**
→→ Promotion in marketing

Online shopping

About a million new shops have appeared around the world since 1993 all located in the same place: the Internet. This virtual world has become a marketer's dream with single-location shops, open 24 hours every day of the year able to sell their goods to everyone with a computer and Internet connection (and maybe a credit card). The Internet has given us reason to completely reconsider the meaning of 'place'.

Exclusive distribution

Only Tiffany sells real Tiffany. They are willing to sell it in stores or online, but the only place to get that light blue box is a real Tiffany outlet. This is true for many products. Consider car brands that sell exclusively through their own owned and operated dealerships, or outdoors outfitters such as L.L. Bean or many fashion brands such as GAP, Banana Republic or Victoria's Secret. Each has chosen as their channel strategy to keep full control of the process and not to seek wider distribution, and therefore sales, of their products.

← What are distribution channels and how do they work?
→ **Distribution strategies**
→→ Developing and managing your sales force

123

Designing your channel strategy

Once you've determined the level of exclusivity you want in your distribution channels, it's time to design your channel strategy.

Evaluate big picture conditions

How will the state of the economy influence your new product introduction (if it is in fact a new product)? How will political events affect the introduction? Are there competitive products, or competitive actions that will have an effect? Evaluate the big picture to determine both the opportunities and the obstacles you are likely to have to deal with.

Analyse competitive channels

We don't work in a vacuum; our competition is eagerly trying to figure out how to get the same customers we are. The better we understand our competition, the better we can design a channel strategy that takes advantage of our strengths and our competition's weaknesses.

Our recent e-commerce studies clearly show an upward trend in global online shopping. While there is growth in nearly all global markets, the lesser developed markets are maturing faster than many of their more developed counterparts. It will not be long before we have a nearly level playing field across the globe.
David Boyd

Define end-user needs and desires

We all work for the end-user of our product and the better we understand that, the better our strategic decisions are likely to be. For our channel strategy to be effective, we need to deliver our brand as our consumers expect and want us to. True lovers of exclusive brands such as Tiffany don't want their brand too available to the public. It's the exclusivity that gives the brand its worth.

Rank your priorities for your channel's partners

When looking for appropriate retailers to sell your product, what do you expect from them? If you are selling something highly technical (such as an advanced digital camera), you might want the retailer to employ highly trained salespeople capable of explaining your product. If it's an everyday item such as canned tomatoes, you might want the retailer to give you special placement or seasonal promotion or even for them to advertise your brand. Do you need your channel to service your product (such as a car dealer or appliance shop)? Make a thorough list of all you want your channel to be able to do and then rank them from most to least important.

Design channel structures

Finally, you've done all your homework. Now it's time to select where you want your product to be sold, put together a package that works for that retailer and implement your channel strategy.

Monitor, evaluate and improve

Nothing is ever perfect in marketing. Immediately upon beginning a channel strategy it's time to monitor your successes and failures, evaluate every partner and step along the way and improve as you go to guarantee the most successful channel strategy possible. Everything can be improved on and nothing you do in marketing is done in a vacuum. Competitors will react and cause you to act and react as well.

124   **The Fundamentals of Marketing**

←← Strategic pricing
➔ **Distribution channel marketing**
→→ Promotion in marketing

Designing a water channel

In the previous chapter we looked at a number of brands of water and how the second most common element on Earth has been successfully branded, over and over again.

So, let's do it now. Our brand of water is called **100MILLIONBC; DINOSAUR WATER.**

We are taking huge sections of ancient glaciers, melting them, purifying them and charging $50.00 for a glass bottle of water that's been frozen since dinosaurs walked the Earth. Advertising promises the water is at least '100 million years fresh' and it's served precisely at 2℃.

Where should you sell it?

Obviously, this water is pretty special, and the supply isn't unlimited. That's why we are charging 25 times what we might change for a normal bottle of water.

At this price, what are our competitors? Actually, not water. At this price, we are most likely to sell only to 1) people who want a once in a lifetime experience or 2) people trying to show off their wealth/success. Our research shows us the second group is a more valuable target for us. What do we know about these people? They are the *nouveau riche*. They like to show off their wealth in very public ways. They probably lack the real style and sophistication of the upper class 'old moneyed' families but may have as much money or more. Where can we find newly minted millionaires in reasonable abundance? Beijing, Shanghai, Moscow, Mumbai and Hollywood. And where do we find them in these cities? At very expensive clubs where people go to be seen. We've just eliminated the need for distributing our product in well over 99% of the potential establishments in the world.

What do we want from our channel partners?

We want them to serve 100MILLIONBC water elegantly at exactly the right temperature. In order to do that we will probably need to supply a special refrigerator unit that keeps the water at 2℃.

So, let's market 100MILLIONBC in the top 50 most exclusive international nightclubs in these five cities where our target market can buy a bottle of 100MILLIONBC to drink between bottles of Cristal champagne. Will they sell it? Absolutely; think of the profit margin!

← What are distribution channels and how do they work?
→ **Distribution strategies**
→ Developing and managing your sales force

125

Understand what your distributors/retailers need

As we saw right at the beginning of this chapter, manufacturers, wholesalers and retailers all want to make as much money as possible from the distribution and sales process. But is there more to the picture? Let's take a look at these middlemen and try to understand what they all really want. Money is part of the story, but only part.

Quality product
Of course they want a quality product. Their reputation is made in part by the products they sell, so the fact that you've made a quality product will be very important to them.

Full menu of product possibilities
Most large retailers don't want to deal with a producer for a single product. With the average hypermarket stocking 150,000 different items, you can imagine what it would be like if every one of them was manufactured by a different manufacturer.

Adequate profit potential
Shelf space in stores is very expensive real estate and anything that sits on them is expected to turnover quickly. What is adequate profit potential? That depends. Retailer margins vary widely from less than 10% for some fast-moving consumer goods to as much as 1,000% for some luxury items such as jewellery. Retailers today are very sophisticated and know exactly how much money they will demand in exchange for shelf space.

Willingness to stand behind the product
It's not good enough to just make a good-quality product; you must also stand behind it with services and guarantees.

Rapid delivery
Time really is money in this business so retailers expect rapid and frequent delivery, minimising how much product they have to hold in inventory. Generally manufacturers in the beer and snacks business will stock the shelves themselves to guarantee the retailer has adequate supply at all times.

Price protection
Prices go up, prices go down. Retailers generally expect to be protected from the possibility of prices going down. Say you've purchased 50,000 cases of shampoo at $50.00 per case. If the price next month changes to $45.00 per case, that retailer has overpaid by $250,000 and will expect a credit of that amount.

Co-op advertising budget
Retailers expect manufacturers to support their brands with advertising that will drive sales. Some manufacturers will share advertising costs with retailers by paying for part of the ad when their brand is featured. Co-op advertising is fairly common with luxury goods manufacturers such as watches. Most of the ads you see for watch brands that include the store names and locations are probably co-op ads.

Competitive end-user pricing
Retailers expect a certain amount of profit per square foot per month. They may not care how many actual items they have to sell, but they will care that they reach the number they need to rationalise the shelf space they are allotting you. The only way to get what they need is with a competitive end-user price. If the product is priced too high, sales will probably not be high enough and the retailer won't make as much as they need to. If there are too many middlemen involved, the end-user price will probably be too high to sell the amount needed.

←← Strategic pricing
➜ **Distribution channel marketing**
→→ Promotion in marketing

New product developments

Retailers want a constant stream of innovation from the manufacturers they work with. This includes new products. Even though 80% of new products fail, new products drive increased retail sales and are critical to retailers growing their overall sales year upon year.

Market knowledge

Retailers expect manufacturers to be experts in their market. Retailers know retail and are very good at what they do. They cannot be experts on every product they handle and rely on manufacturers' sales representatives to understand the market well enough to help them grow.

Payment terms

Once again time is money. A manufacturer that will allow the retailer additional time to pay could actually be increasing the profitability of the relationship. Generally, manufacturers expect to be paid within 30 days and often offer financial incentives for prompt payment.

Private/generic label equivalents

Most successful brands have a private or generic label equivalent. These are often, but not always, made by the same manufacturer.

Build store traffic

Store traffic is what retailers call the number of potential customers that pass through their doors.

Sales training/free product literature

Retailers will want someone to train their own salespeople especially when it comes to highly technical products.

Territorial integrity

Retailers love exclusivity. If you are the only store that handles a hot new product, you are nearly guaranteed to have customers lined up to buy the item. The level of exclusivity is negotiated between the marketer/manufacturer and the retailer. Sometimes brands are renamed with few or no actual product changes and sold 'exclusively' by two different store chains. For example, it's nearly impossible to compare prices on mattresses. Why? Because the same mattress model is given multiple names, multiple different overlay fabrics and then sold in multiple stores. It's exactly the same mattress, but these subtle changes are made to prevent comparison pricing.

Efficient stock management/ regional warehousing

Along with rapid delivery, retailers want to minimise their stocking and inventory costs so they need their suppliers to have efficient stock management.

Manufacturer's reputation

As the old cliché says, you are known by the company you keep. This is true of retailers as well.

Demonstration items at reduced cost

If sales of your product require demonstration, retailers will want those demonstration items at little or no cost.

← What are distribution channels and how do they work?
→ **Distribution strategies**
→→ Developing and managing your sales force

127

Developing and managing your sales force

Your sales force is your lifeline in the distribution channel. You can have the best product at the best price with the best advertising campaign supporting it, but if the sales force doesn't get it right in-store it's all a waste. Procter & Gamble find this part of marketing so important that they split their marketing department into national and local business units with the local units responsible for 'winning in-store'.

A great sales force can almost create miracles and an inferior one can prove the weak link that allows everything to fall apart at the shop level. It's why the sales team is one of the highest-paid sectors in the entire chain of command.

As marketing manager, the sales force may or may not report to you. Chances are they don't. This creates one of the worst management situations where you have all the responsibility and no authority to guarantee things get done properly. This situation arises because many companies share their sales force between many different brands, all vying for the salespeople's time and attention. Management can't make a sales force report equally to ten marketing managers so they normally determine another structure. A common solution is to have all sales and marketing staff ultimately reporting to the same high-level manager.

Developing your sales force

Hiring a sales force can be one of the most crucial steps in a brand's success. Many companies want experienced salespeople with established contacts who can hit the ground selling from day one. Some companies prefer to train their salespeople from scratch and only promote from within. Whichever is right for you depends on your goals and your resources. If you can afford to train your sales force from start to finish, there is more control and consistency in doing business that way.

In hiring salespeople, whether new or experienced, you are looking for people driven by achieving goals, team players who are quick to share the glory and pain and people of the highest ethical standards. The stereotypical salesman who will get a sale at any cost wouldn't last in the world of professional marketing. Sales success is all about reaching stretch-goals, doing things no one thought possible and developing strong long-term relationships built on trust and service.

128   The Fundamentals of Marketing

←← Strategic pricing
→ **Distribution channel marketing**
→→ Promotion in marketing

Geographic set-up, by product or by market

One thing you will need to decide is how to design the sales territory to eliminate overlap between competing salespeople. There are many ways to do this, the most common being geographic boundaries. One salesperson handles one section of the country, another handles another section. Some companies prefer to set up boundaries by product. Salesperson A sells Product X all over the country and Salesperson B sells Product Y all over the country. Another popular way to divide responsibilities is by market. Salesperson A handles all national accounts; Salesperson B handles regional and local businesses. In reality, large sales organisations generally use a variety of boundaries for any one product.

Managing

Once you've hired your sales force and set boundaries for each member of the team, it's time to train and motivate them to do what you want. At best you become the coach of a sports team setting goals and designing tactics to help the athletes succeed.

Training

Training isn't just about showing people how to do their jobs well; it's about motivation and management. Training can be motivational in that you are showing people how to achieve more; whether in their financial goals or simply a feeling of accomplishment. Training can also be a management tool in that employees who believe they don't know everything you know will want to stick around to learn more. Salespeople are motivated by being in the game at all times and being well-rewarded for their success. They also have a tendency to jump ship to the highest bidder if they aren't properly cared for.

Set motivational objectives

A motivational objective is a goal that on the surface appears just a bit too far away to achieve by regular means. It can't be too unreachable or it will fail to motivate. However, if the salesperson sees the goal as possible, they are likely to use their best effort to reach it.

Possible rewards

In all of business, you are asking people to reach beyond their natural abilities and normal workload to accomplish your goals. Why should they? Because in doing so, they will receive exceptional rewards. The goals must seem possible and the rewards must seem worth the effort. Money is the obvious reward. However, rewards can include additional vacation, trips, promotions, recognition, awards or company cars.

Clear administrative policy

Although you've done your best to hire people of great personal integrity, you want clear administrative policy that leaves no room for interpretation in the field on the spot. What are your company's financial terms? What does your company do if a client falls behind in payments? You can easily see the chaos that could ensue if you didn't have clear and simple policies to cover these eventualities.

129

← Distribution strategies
→ **Developing and managing your sales force**
→→ Customer relationship marketing (CRM)

Logistics

Logistical management is a growing field within marketing and a huge source of cost. It is also an area that many marketers are now discovering can lead to great cost savings. Wal-Mart's success globally is due to many smart moves, but none quite as important as their superior logistical management. Wal-Mart was one of the first companies to study logistical management with an eye to reducing costs at the same time as increasing efficiency. Like the airline industry, Wal-Mart adopted hubs where products could be stored and shipped to the stores as they were needed. These hubs directly monitor store sales, using barcode scanner data to anticipate when and how much shampoo, vitamins and so on will be required by each store. Using this system, Wal-Mart found huge cost savings in logistics management which they were able (at least in part) to pass along to consumers in the form of lower prices, giving them a clear competitive advantage against their competition.

All commodity volume

Marketers use a measurement called ACV (all commodity volume) to measure distribution in relation to sales. If a brand has 80% ACV, that product is available in shops that are responsible for 80% of the category sales. If you tell me your product is available in two shops or 20,000 stores, it means almost nothing. If you tell me your product has 80% ACV, I know your product is available in shops responsible for 80% of category volume – therefore you have adequate channel distribution.

Time and money – shipping costs

I once heard a very senior marketing manager say that everything was either 'time or money; if you have enough of one, the other goes down, if you don't, it goes up'. While quite simplistic, it's also surprisingly true.

How you ship goods will add a little or a lot to the overall cost of goods people end up paying in the store. How you ship will also add a little or a lot to the time required to move items from one place to another. The shipping costs of a product can cost from 1% of the retail price to over 50% depending on time and money. Let's take a look at some of the freight options:

Air freight

This is generally the fastest and most expensive for moving items great distances.

Truck

Trucking is probably the second fastest, most versatile and second most expensive way to move goods around the world. Obviously trucking is necessary for store delivery, but it can become a very inefficient way to get from a manufacturer to the store.

Rail

If your country has adequate infrastructure for rail transport, rail can be a very efficient method of shipping goods across country.

Water

While slow, sea freight can be a very cost-efficient way of transporting goods. Once the goods reach the shores of its intended country, further shipment depends either on inland waterways or changing shipping methods.

Pipeline

Products such as oil and natural gas are often shipped via pipeline. While the infrastructure cost is very high, pipeline can pump a tremendous amount of product long distances for less than any other method on an ongoing basis.

←← Strategic pricing
➜ **Distribution channel marketing**
→→ Promotion in marketing

What typically goes wrong in distribution/ channel marketing?

Learning from experience so that you don't repeat the same mistakes made by your predecessors is always a good idea. Here are some common mistakes that channel managers make that can doom the entire marketing effort.

Ignoring the end-user

It's very easy and even common for channel managers to get so tied up in their world that they forget the end-user of the product. Remember, salespeople sell to buyers at retail stores, neither of whom have any natural connection to the end-user. The problems come when people not in touch with end-users are trying to design programmes aimed at attracting end-users. If an end-user is tiring of a certain brand then the channel manager might not know until it's too late.

Expecting retailers to bend to your will

As discussed in the very brief history of marketing section of Chapter 1, manufacturers once held all the power in the relationship – until scanners came along. Once retailers were armed with scanner data that showed exactly what was selling, where and when – they had more information and therefore more power than the manufacturer. Large retailers began to exercise that power by delisting slow-moving product and planning shelves to match sales. At first manufacturers resisted giving up the power, but the wise ones understood (after a few false starts) that life had fundamentally changed and would never be quite the same again. Those companies embraced the new reality and found ways to make it work. Retailers sell your product, or they don't. If you expect them to do exactly as you wish, you may be in for a tough sales season.

Sticking with one channel too long

Marketers get used to doing business in one way and are reluctant to change. Change for the sake of change is rarely helpful and generally just an added cost. However, change for the better (constantly looking for efficiencies and better ways of doing business) can be a huge competitive advantage.

Basing decisions on relationships over business objectives

It's common for salespeople with long-term relationships to start making decisions based on those relationships. While you don't want to be heartless to people you have long-term relationships with, business is business and it's best to remain focused on achieving your business objectives.

Focusing on too few channels of distribution

While selling to fewer channels can greatly simplify your life, the more sales are spread at a variety of types of shops, the more you are likely to need a broader strategy. For example, if you want to sell disposable diapers in the US, selling to Wal-Mart alone will get you into stores that represent roughly 75% of category sales. However, if you are selling milk, Wal-Mart is a relatively minor player and you will need many more channels of distribution.

Customer relationship marketing (CRM)

In the 1990s, marketers discovered relationships and their importance to long-term success. Brands such as Toyota, Lexus, Honda, Apple, Nike, and Sony had built relationships with their users that paid huge dividends even in tough times. A current Toyota owner is about ten times more likely to make their next purchase a Toyota than the owner of a Ford or General Motors car. It goes well beyond brand loyalty into an active two-way relationship

There is little doubt that relevant and timely e-mail communications are becoming ever more central to the development of successful integrated marketing programs that build and accelerate long-term profitable customer relationships.
Al DiGuido

that turns owners from customers into brand evangelists. After all, there is nothing more effective in marketing that a good friend telling you how tremendous a certain brand is. Talk to Facebook users about their Facebook and you'll see the most enthusiastic and passionate group of people that want to convert their non-Facebook-using friends. This all happens when a brand builds a strong and two-way relationship with its user. Relationships like this occur both at the retail level (between the marketer/manufacturer and their retailers) and at the end-user level and must be effectively managed and developed.

Retail level relationships
Remember, at the end of the day if your brand isn't available in the right stores at the right price and time, you simply aren't going to succeed. Now put yourself in the shoes of the retailer. This person is likely to be happy to build a strong working relationship with you, but you need to realise there are literally hundreds of brands trying to build these relationships.

132   **The Fundamentals of Marketing**

←← Strategic pricing
➜ **Distribution channel marketing**
⇢ Promotion in marketing

Establishing relationships

This isn't about friendship; it's about helping retailers succeed and thereby helping you succeed at the same time. Keep in mind that the retailer has literally hundreds of people begging for their time. Not wasting their time, but constantly bringing information that will build their business sets a mutually profitable relationship in motion and is a show of respect.

Market visits

Everyone intends to do what is promised, but business has plenty of chaos that can easily get in the way. The best way to know what's going on is simply to look. So, you'll want to make regular unannounced market visits to make sure everything is in fact going as planned (and paid for).

Advisory council

You may want to develop an advisory council of different sized retailers that can keep you apprised of how your efforts and policies are affecting sales in the market.

Sales force management and channel audits

Just managing your sales force can be a tremendous challenge in itself. Sales managers generally refer to it as herding cats because salespeople in general are very independently minded, even the best of the team players. It is likely that your sales force has more than 20 different items that they are responsible for selling. We would be tremendously naive to think that salespeople will handle every product equally. Why do you believe they should pay attention to your brand? Make sure you communicate that belief and the reasons for it to your sales force.

Managing channel conflict

No matter how much you try to design the conflict out of the system, with this many different handlers there will be conflict. Clear objectives and policies for handling conflict will go a long way to smooth the journey from manufacturer to end-user.

End-user level relationships

Establishing end-user customer relationships isn't really all that different from establishing friendships or romantic relationships. Think about the qualities of a best friend or spouse and come up with the equivalent in business and you are well on your way to establishing a relationship based on trust and even love.

Using end-users to make you better

By creating a two-way dialogue, you can actually get your end-users to help you make better products. You want a stronger and better brand and so do those who love you. Together, imagine what you can achieve!

Real and fake relationships

When customer relationship marketing became popular, everyone jumped in as quickly as they could. However, most marketing people didn't actually want real relationships with consumers; they wanted to tick off the box and convince their bosses they built relationships with their consumers. Real relationships will strengthen a brand; fake ones can actually weaken a brand as you are living under the belief you are in touch with your customer.

Legal and ethical considerations

There are laws and ethical considerations around the world that guide and attempt to keep commerce fair for all. Here is a basic list of the major ones to help you understand the atmosphere we all work in.

→ **Collusion:** It is illegal for two or more marketers to collude together against another marketer in a way which could do harm to that third party.

→ **Price discrimination:** It is illegal to charge different prices to different channels unless those prices are based on the cost of doing business (for example, quantity discounts).

→ **Price fixing:** It is illegal for competitors to get together and set prices.

← Developing and managing your sales force
→ **Customer relationship marketing (CRM)**
→→ Case study: Wal-Mart

133

Case study: Wal-Mart

In 1962 a retailer named Sam Walton opened his first Wal-Mart store. Walton saw a new trend of discount stores and wanted to get into the business early. That same year, K-Mart and Target stores were also launched.

Thinking differently

Walton didn't have the deep pockets to invest in discount retailing that his competitors had, so he had to do things differently. Since Walton set up Wal-Mart in rural Arkansas, major manufacturers refused to truck goods to his small stores. So, he set up his own distribution centres and his own trucking company. He also eliminated all the middlemen by travelling to major manufacturers to do business directly and thus significantly cut costs. Walton created the concept of 'Everyday Low Price' (EDLP) to smooth out the rollercoaster nature of retail demand based on sales. This also allowed him to minimise advertising expenditures because there weren't temporary sales to drive traffic; his goods cost less than his competition every day. As stores multiplied, Walton would choose rural locations between two small to medium-sized cities. While

Wal-Mart around the world

Wal-Mart is the largest private employer in the world; it operates in Mexico as Walmex, in the UK as ASDA, and in Japan as Seiyu. It also has wholly owned operations in Argentina, Brazil, Canada, and Puerto Rico.

⇇ Strategic pricing
➡ **Distribution channel marketing**
⇉ Promotion in marketing

his competition was focused on the large cities, Walton was building his empire in two markets they wouldn't get to for years.

He also invented the 'hub and spoke' design of centralised distribution centres. Today in the US 114 distribution centres serve nearly 4,000 stores with over 75,000 people working just in the logistics group trying to make their distribution systems more and more efficient.

Walton computerised his inventory in the early 1960s and enrolled in an IBM computer class in upstate New York for the sole purpose of hiring the smartest student in the class to computerise his stores. With the advent of UPC scanners Wal-Mart created the most sophisticated logistics system in retail history with a system that told store personnel and the regional distribution warehouse exactly what inventory was available and what was needed in each store. In 1989 Wal-Mart's distribution costs were 1.7% of sales compared with 3.5% for K-Mart. That might not sound like a lot, but with Wal-Mart's huge sales it could represent savings of about $4.5 billion annually.

Wal-Mart's single-minded focus on being the lowest-priced store in the world has led to tremendous innovation throughout retailing, Walton and his Wal-Mart team have built the strongest organisation and most efficient distribution in the world.

Today, Wal-Mart is the world's largest retailer and has over two million employees worldwide. There are 6,500 stores serving an estimated 138 million customers weekly. Wal-Mart carries a broad assortment of brand name and private label merchandise from clothing to small appliances, house wares and even grocery stores in their Super-Centres. Their membership-only warehouse stores known as Sam's Club sell to small business owners as well as consumers buying in bulk, and their new smaller Neighbourhood Markets are reinventing the local grocery store with the same EDLP philosophy.

Sam Walton was named Richest Man in America by *Forbes* magazine in 1985 and remained there until his death from cancer at age 74. He left his money to his wife and children, creating five of America's richest people – all from a single store and a vision of what he could create.

Moral of the story

Look for every opportunity to become more efficient. Not many university students plan on someday becoming a logistics manager; it doesn't seem very exciting. However, as we've seen with Wal-Mart, logistics and distribution management can be the key to beating your competitors. By fundamentally changing the costs of distribution, Wal-Mart were able to save billions of dollars which they could pass along to their customers with lower prices than their competition. The contest is over; Wal-Mart won. K-Mart lost, JC Penney lost and Target decided to change their tactics and win a much smaller game. In what may have been one of the strangest news stories ever, Wal-Mart was credited by every major news outlet in the US with keeping America out of recession during the late 1990s. The everyday low prices kept people buying which kept the economy churning. It's not just about the company's bottom line, but in this case about the entire country's bottom line. Wal-Mart's innovations have greatly improved distribution management throughout the retail industry. Every 'P' in marketing offers opportunity!

←← Customer relationship marketing (CRM)
→ **Case study: Wal-Mart**
→→ Smart plan: Part five

135

Smart plan: Part five

So, where should we sell our new battery? The same product placed in either a large supermarket, a specialist technology shop or a local pharmacy will be a very different brand and will therefore be successful at different price points and will have very different sales. Let's design a basic channel marketing strategy for the Smart Battery and see how we should go to market.

Smart battery: Exercise two

1) Do you think you should introduce the Smart Battery through direct channels, indirect channels or through some combination of the two? Why?
2) Do you want your Smart Battery to have ubiquitous, selective or exclusive distribution? Why is that right for your new brand?
3) What big picture events will help and hurt the sale of the Smart Battery (for example economic trends, political trends or environmental trends)?
4) What actions do you expect from your competitors Duracell, Energizer and Panasonic? Why do you expect them to behave in this way?
5) Identify three of your competition's major strengths and three weaknesses.
6) List everything you need your channel partners to do for the introduction of this battery and then rank them from most to least important.
7) What does your end-user want from this battery?
8) Design your proposed distribution structure.
9) Discuss your strategy with a professional in the retail trade.
10) Describe your sales force plan.

136   The Fundamentals of Marketing

← Strategic pricing
→ Distribution channel marketing
→→ Promotion in marketing

Anticipating competitive moves

What do you think your competition will do? Let's analyse them in order to predict their probable moves.

1) What is their marketing mix? Understand their product's strengths and weaknesses, their pricing, their channel strategy and their promotion plan both in terms of size and scope.

2) Speed can be a tremendous competitive advantage in marketing. How long do you think it will take your competitors them to get a rival Smart Battery to market? Bear in mind that after Apple introduced the iPhone, Nokia, LG and Samsung all had their touch-screen version of the iPhone out within about four months.

3) We've set our objectives and strategies for our product launch; what are our competitor's objectives and strategies?

4) What are our competitors really good at, and what aren't they so good at?

5) Are we a significant threat to our competitors? Do they think we are, or even recognise our strengths and potential? How would this affect their response?

6) Consider their market position and performance changes: how important are they really? Have they been growing or declining?

7) Retailers want to know that marketers are constantly expanding and improving your product line. How about your competitors? How innovative are they? What product enhancements or improvements are likely in their pipeline of innovation?

8) Consider strategic intelligence, how much do your competitors really know and understand about their end-user? Do they consistently look for ways to delight consumers or are they satisfied with the status quo?

9) Do we question our competitors ethics as a company or can we count on their ethics? In every business there are a variety of manufacturers with a wide range of ethical standards. Where does each of our competitors lie?

10) What do end-users think of our competitors? Are they passionate about the brand, or do they have almost no opinion about it?

Chapter questions and exercises

1 **Find three examples of ubiquitous distribution, selective distribution and exclusive distribution. Why was this the right distribution strategy for each of these brands?**

2 **What do you think would happen to a selective distribution brand like Godiva chocolates if they suddenly decided to become ubiquitous? How might they do it and still remain successful?**

3 **How do you think you could effectively build relationships with end-user customers?**

Promotion in marketing

Marlboro Cigarettes

Marlboro is possibly the world's best marketing success story. The product may be 'just a cigarette', but the brand defines much of what is good and pure about the American West.

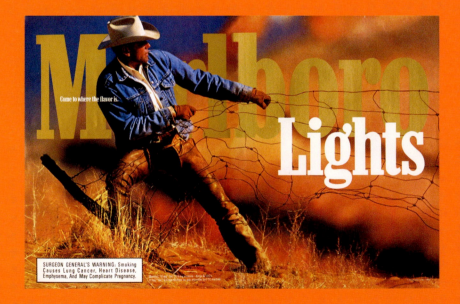

Come to where the flavor is.

Marlboro Lights

SURGEON GENERAL'S WARNING: Smoking Causes Lung Cancer, Heart Disease, Emphysema, And May Complicate Pregnancy.

You've made it to your last 'P': Promotion. Promotion includes any efforts you use to promote your brand including advertising, public relations, sales promotion, event marketing, sports marketing, guerrilla marketing, buzz marketing, sponsorship, product placement, merchandising, in-store activities, personal sales, mobile marketing and more. By now, you've probably gained a real appreciation for both the complexity and breadth of a marketing manager's job.

Let's jump right in and take a look at how marketing communications actually work.

Chapter 6 will help you:

→ **Understand how marketing professionals create promotional messages.**
→ **Understand how ad agencies work.**
→ **Write creative briefs.**
→ **Understand the 'big ideas' in advertising.**

The basic theories

Most communications theorists overcomplicate how communications actually work. Anyone who has ever spoken to another person or written a note knows intuitively how basic communications work. At its most basic level, there is a sender, a receiver and the message itself. I write this book, you read it; that's it.

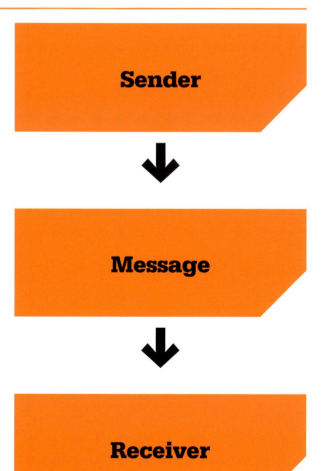

Fig. 6-1: Basic communication
In modelling communications, you can discover both opportunities and obstacles in getting yourself heard and understood. This very basic model assumes there is only you and me and whatever I want to tell you, you will hear and understand.

Interference

But is that really how communications occur? What else are you doing right now? The Internet, your friends, your phone, your television, iPod, stereo and much more could be competing with this book for your attention right now. It is more than likely that you are listening to your iPod, instant messaging friends or even have the TV on in the background while you are trying to read this. All these are competing for your attention (and just by me mentioning them, you've reconsidered each of them). We call these interference or noise. So the model becomes a little more complicated.

In Figure 6-2, note that both sender and receiver experience some level of interference. As the sender, my choice of language or medium may actually help or hinder the message from being received as I intend, while on your end, there are plenty of distractions competing for your attention and comprehension.

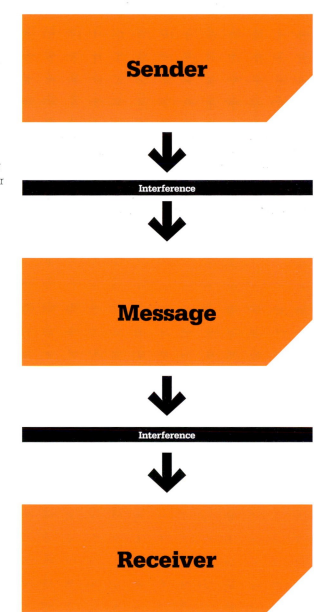

Fig. 6-2: Interference
Consider everything that is competing for your attention right now. TVs, iPods, computer screens, telephones may all be causing interference between what I want to say and your ability to hear and comprehend the message.

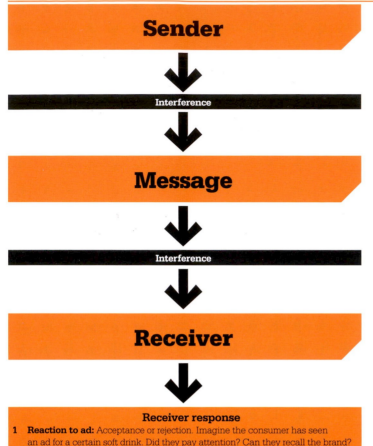

Sender

Interference

Message

Interference

Receiver

Receiver response

1 **Reaction to ad:** Acceptance or rejection. Imagine the consumer has seen an ad for a certain soft drink. Did they pay attention? Can they recall the brand? Can they recall what the ad was trying to say? Did they believe it? Did they care about it?
2 **Learning:** Was there information the consumer didn't already know? What are they going to do with that information?
3 **Acknowledgement of category need:** If the consumer is out of soft drinks, a well-crafted Coke commercial may make them recognise and acknowledge their need for the category. The brand preference isn't yet acknowledged, only the category of product.
4 **Multiple brand awareness:** The consumer may then go on to think "I need a drink. What brands do I usually buy? I buy Coke, Dr Pepper, Jones soda and Orange Crush."
5 **Brand preference:** 'All things being equal, I'll always take a Dr Pepper.'
6 **Brand experience:** 'Every time I have one, I feel refreshed and I'm glad I'm drinking something unique. Only Dr Pepper tastes like Dr Pepper.'
7 **Search and evaluation:** 'Where is Dr Pepper, and how much is it compared to the other brands I also like?'
8 **Purchase:** 'I bought Dr Pepper.'
9 **Use:** 'I'm drinking Dr Pepper.'
10 **Post use evaluation.** 'I still think this is the best soft drink on the market!'

Marketing communications

The next level of complexity is marketing communications. With marketing communications, the sender is trying to get you to take some sort of action and probably spend money. Therefore, the model follows the pattern shown in Figure 6-3.

Fig. 6-3: Marketing communications
While the chart becomes more and more complicated, it's all still pretty much common sense that we have a sender, a receiver, interference and there is a logical customer purchase sequence to move to action.

142   **The Fundamentals of Marketing**

←← Distribution channel marketing
→ **Promotion in marketing**
→→ Appendix

Your marketing communications depend on your target

Keep in mind that not all customers are created equal. A sophisticated marketer will actually place a value on different consumer groups based on their return on investment.

Your most valuable customer is one loyal to your brand. They use your brand exclusively and depending on their level of passion, may actually contribute to building the brand by converting their family and friends.

Your next most valuable consumer is the multiple brand switcher. They use your product with some degree of regularity, but it is part of an acceptable set of brands they tend to switch between. For whatever reason, your brand is not seen as the very best (or, they simply like some variety in their lives).

The third most valuable group is your competitor's brand loyal users. They have demonstrated a liking for the category, but for some reason have chosen one of your competitors to your brand. 'Brand loyal' doesn't mean these people can't be converted to your brand. It simply means for the time being, they prefer another brand.

The next most valuable group is the category users with no loyalty. They use your product category, but for whatever reason (often price shopping) haven't built any loyalty to any particular brand.

And the final group is the non-category users, meaning that they don't currently use any product in the category. These non-category users wouldn't seem to be a valuable target, but they are often the source of future growth. Consider the sports car category. You may not want a sports car with toddlers running around the house, but the second you can get rid of the MPV, you are a strong potential customer for the category.

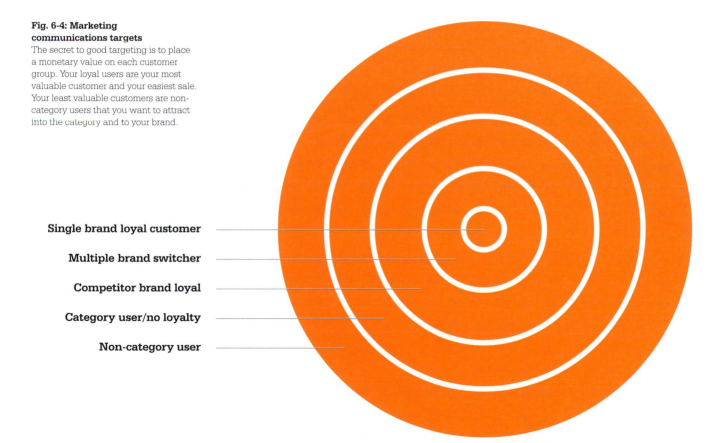

Fig. 6-4: Marketing communications targets
The secret to good targeting is to place a monetary value on each customer group. Your loyal users are your most valuable customer and your easiest sale. Your least valuable customers are non-category users that you want to attract into the category and to your brand.

Single brand loyal customer

Multiple brand switcher

Competitor brand loyal

Category user/no loyalty

Non-category user

Rational versus emotional selling

Two of the largest manufacturers in the world, Procter & Gamble and Philip Morris, couldn't market much more differently from each other.

P&G relies mostly on very rational selling. Their detergents get out stains other detergents leave behind. Pampers keep your baby drier. Pantene leaves your hair looking healthier. Oil of Olay leaves your skin looking younger. Notice the collection of 'er' words: cleaner, drier, healthier and younger. P&G has traditionally relied on rational selling with product superiority. There is certainly nothing wrong with that! This approach has worked well for decades, however as competitors' products are continually improving P&G are in an increasingly vulnerable position.

Now consider Philip Morris. Is Marlboro the best cigarette in the world? Who knows? Unlike stain removal, cigarette preference is hard to measure. Blind tests show they all pretty much taste and smoke alike. All are approximately the same length, made with the same tobacco, and the same type of filter, wrapping and so on. So what's different? The marketing. Ask a loyal Marlboro smoker and they'll tell you theirs is the best-tasting cigarette in the world. However, it's likely that if you give them a different brand to smoke – they'll never even know it isn't a Marlboro unless you tell them or show them. But the pack, the positioning of the brand, the imagery around the brand, its advertising, promotions and pricing all evoke the masculine independence of the old West as a way to attract new smokers and hold their loyal smokers. If, like Philip Morris, you have little to say, or maybe legally little you can say about your product, you are forced into 100% pure marketing. Philip Morris therefore uses emotional branding to build one of the top ten most valuable brands in the world.

Consider other brands that rely on emotional branding to build strong emotional bonds with their users: Starbucks, Red Bull, Coca-Cola, Nike, and Apple. Are these superior products? Sometimes. But they are nearly always superior brands.

Rational branding is easier, and if you have a truly superior product that consumers agree is clearly superior, plus a reasonable reason to believe you are going to keep that superiority, then rational branding is probably enough. But, if you are like over 99% of brands on the market today and perform at parity with your competitors, or your superiority isn't abundantly clear to the majority of the population (like Apple computers), or you believe your state of superiority is probably a temporary status, you are going to need to build a bond with your consumers that goes beyond the rational into the emotional level.

144   The Fundamentals of Marketing

⇚ Distribution channel marketing
➔ Promotion in marketing
⇉ Appendix

Turning ordinary customers into brand evangelists

Consumers today define themselves by the brands they use. Many Apple Macintosh users are more like a cult than a consumer group. Talk to a Mac user and you'll find an elitist group that nearly worships their messianic founder (Steve Jobs). They often believe that they are a little smarter and more creative than the rest of the population. They use only Apple products, hang out in Apple stores as though it were a lounge, communicate to other 'members of the club' with e-mail that goes to mac.com, and wear their passion for the brand in clothing and any product Apple introduces. That's more than a relationship; it's a love affair, a passion, even an obsession.

Kevin Roberts, CEO of Saatchi & Saatchi Advertising, has coined the word 'lovemarks' to explain brands we are loyal to 'beyond reason'. The Leo Burnett Company studied brand believers; those so passionate about brands that they become brand evangelists. No matter what we call it, having people so passionate about your brand that they bring in more converts can only be smart business.

It's not enough to just put your product up for sale and hope for the best. In today's market you must work to build a relationship with your consumer. A strong relationship with your consumer means they will prefer your brand to others (brand preference) and that whenever possible they will always use your brand instead of others (brand loyalty). Since keeping loyal customers costs far less than acquiring new ones, it's in your own self-interest to make sure consumers fall in love with your brand.

Lovemarks transcend brands. They deliver beyond your expectations of great performance. Like great brands, they sit on top of high levels of respect – but there the similarities end.

Lovemarks reach your heart as well as your mind, creating an intimate, emotional connection that you just can't live without. Ever.

Take a brand away and people will find a replacement. Take a Lovemark away and people will protest its absence. Lovemarks are a relationship, not a mere transaction. You don't just buy Lovemarks, you embrace them passionately. That's why you never want to let go.

Kevin Roberts, lovemarks.com

←← The basic theories
➜ Rational versus emotional selling
→→ The communications revolution

145

The communications revolution

A great deal of time and energy has been spent recently in discussing the changing communications industry. Although the industry is undeniably changing, it could be argued that except for a few periods of lull in the past several hundred years, it always has been in a state of flux and always will be.

Why is this important? Because the communications industry works by predicting future developments; it is only by understanding what is happening now and why it is happening in that way, that you will you be able to see where the business is going and get there before your competition.

The marketing communications business is slightly over 300 years old. The first newspaper advert appeared in 1704. Advertising agencies date back to 1843 when Volley Palmer opened their doors in Philadelphia. Coke didn't register their trademark until 1893, and another Philadelphia agency, N.W. Ayer, opened the first ever 'business-getting department' in 1900. The first pre-recorded TV commercial appeared in 1956 and the Internet as we now know it has only been around since 1993. In the grand scheme of things, this is a very short history to go from a newspaper ad to today's cluttered advertising environment.

Changes in the communications industry

So what is causing the changes today? Let's take a look at the biggest changes in the last decade to get a hint of where this business is going.

Explosion of media vehicles, globalisation and dwindling audience size

In most countries, cable and satellite television pushed broadcast media offerings from three to four major networks in the 1970s and 1980s to hundreds of broadcast offerings from all around the world today. During that period the television-watching audience has grown only slightly both in terms of numbers and number of hours watched. The net effect of this explosion of options for a limited audience is a splintering of viewership over a wider variety of media outlets. In this climate, even the most popular shows have audiences smaller than the below-average shows of the 1970s. People are simply watching a larger variety of programming today. At the same time, the cost of producing elaborate shows has gone up and television networks are charging advertisers more and more for fewer and fewer viewers.

146   The Fundamentals of Marketing

←← Distribution channel marketing
→ **Promotion in marketing**
→› Appendix

And this pattern is not just affecting television. There are hundreds of newspapers available in large cities on the international, national, regional and local level. There are also thousands of magazines, radio stations and unlimited sites on the Internet. As consumers get more choices, so do advertisers.

And what's happened to the 'old media' (such as the original TV networks that used to dominate our screens)? They have declined in effectiveness while their costs continue to rise. One of the reasons you've seen the rise in reality shows is simply down to finances: they're cheaper to produce. The big networks continue their downward slide while advertisers become more and more frustrated with declining audiences and increasing costs.

Explosion of clutter in advertising

One of the main ways in which large media outlets have dealt with dwindling audience numbers, and therefore dwindling revenue, is by increasing the number of commercials they run per hour. In the US, network TV runs 22 minutes of commercials per hour in prime time, local radio stations run up to 40 minutes of advertising per hour and your average fashion magazine is up to 75% advertising. What's the effect of all this advertising? Consumers, for the first time in history, are showing they are willing to pay to avoid advertising with non-commercial stations such as HBO, satellite radio and even magazines that carry no advertising. Consumers have also found ways to avoid advertising with technology such as TiVo and Sky Plus and digital video recorders, which can fast-forward or even jump over commercials altogether. The harder advertisers try to reach us, the harder we work to avoid them.

The Saatchi brothers

Maurice and Charles Saatchi started an advertising agency in London in the 1970s. Along with their finance director, Martin Sorrel (now CEO of WPP), they acquired agency after agency until their 1984 acquisition of the largest advertising agency in the world, Ted Bates, made Saatchi & Saatchi the number one agency in the world. The Saatchi brothers were eventually fired from their own publicly held company and started a competitive agency in London named M&C Saatchi. Ted Bates, the number one advertising agency in the world in 1984, quietly closed their doors in 2005. What is the moral of the story? This is a very dynamic and quick-changing business.

←← Rational versus emotional selling
→ **The communications revolution**
→→→ Developing marketing communications

147

Clients buying advertising agency services à la carte

Only about a decade ago most clients gave agencies their entire account. Today, creative development is at one agency, media planning is at another, media buying may be at yet another and even 'research and planning' could be at a different agency. While all of the top 20 agencies in the world are full-service agencies, clients are buying services independently and competitively.

Fusion of advertising, editorial and entertainment

As consumers find ways to avoid advertisers, advertisers are finding more and more ways to hide their ads by placing them in movies, television shows, and even novels (Bulgari had a novel written whose main plot took place inside a Bulgari store). Watch the James Bond film *Casino Royale* and you'll see 007 using Sony products (GPS, notebook computers), you'll see him driving Ford products, you'll hear him state that he doesn't wear a Rolex watch, but an Omega watch. Make no mistake about it, these are all commercials.

A few smart advertising people realised a decade ago that the entire world was a potential advertising medium limited only by our imagination.

HBO (Home Box Office)

HBO is a subscription-only service and does not carry normal commercials; it broadcasts to over 38 million US subscribers who are all willing to pay extra to avoid advertisements and for quality programming, such as *The Sopranos*.

148   **The Fundamentals of Marketing**

↞ Distribution channel marketing
➜ **Promotion in marketing**
↠ Appendix

Changing technology

Technology has fundamentally changed the way we communicate. While today's teens have never known a world without the Internet, it only dates back to 1993. We spend more time on social networking sites such as Facebook, MySpace and LinkedIn collecting friends (go ahead, find my page), rating our friends and building virtual worlds where we reign supreme than we do actually talking to live human beings. YouTube allows us to perform for the world and possibly become famous (an attribute American teens claim they would prefer to being smart). Then we have a choice of about a billion websites around the world that will entertain us about anything we can possibly think of (and quite a few we never thought of).

Want to watch television? Choose between the 500 channels on your satellite TV, or playback whatever you'd like on TiVo with commercials deleted or just watch them online (such as the BBC's iPlayer), on your iPod, on your phone or PDA or basically anything with a screen. Radio? That's gone satellite as well as terrestrial with nearly unlimited options with no legal oversight. Anything is possible and available.

Do you like avoiding advertising? Do you ever go on the Internet? It's about 90% advertising. Burger King and their brilliant advertising agency Crispin Porter + Bogusky (and The Barbarian Group) developed a silly interactive chicken called subservient chicken <www.subservientchicken. com> in 2004. To demonstrate the Burger King strategy of 'have it your way', the chicken (or large man in chicken suit) will do whatever you tell him to do (with a few limitations).

While crude by today's standards, this was one of the first successful examples an ad agency creating content for their client and for the Internet. By the end of the first day, the site had over one million hits, and 20 million over the first week. One year into the site being up, 14 million unique visitors had visited the site 400 million times in total. That's right – all these people were actually seeking out a Burger King ad and watching it over and over and over. Isn't subservient chicken yesterday's news? It was yesterday's news a month into the programme, but the point is that technology has allowed us to create content that consumers will actually seek out to play with over and over.

Addressable advertising

Within this decade we will have addressable advertising. If I were advertising Pampers, why would I want my commercials going to homes without infants and toddlers? If I were advertising Corona beer, wouldn't I want to target a very specific group of men? If I were trying to sell Audis, wouldn't I want a very specific customer most likely to consider and buy an Audi? Of course I would. As more and more data is collected on our viewing and shopping habits, advertisers are taking a big lesson from the direct mail industry in figuring out how to narrowly target their most likely buyers.

Good marketing communications work in much the same way as any other good communications work: by knowing what you want to say, to whom and then finding a clear and memorable way in which to say it.

←← Rational versus emotional selling
→ **The communications revolution**
→→ Developing marketing communications

149

Developing marketing communications

You've almost arrived at the point where you can begin developing marketing communications. But first we'll take a peek inside advertising agencies, marketing services companies and marketers to see how they develop the work you see in magazines, on television and on the Internet.

How marketing organisations work

There are over 25,000 advertising agencies in the US alone. This includes everything from a single person that does it all to full-service marketing communications companies with several thousand employees under one roof.

Normally, with a major marketer, there are up to eight groups of people involved in developing marketing communications in a full-service marketing communications company, they are:

The client

This is the manufacturer/marketer of a product or service that hires individuals or a company to create and manage marketing communications for them. They participate in strategy development and judge and approve marketing communications but they do not actually develop the communications themselves; the client is often the brand manager who is charged with the overall management of the brand.

Account management

The account manager works directly with the client and is tasked with the management of marketing communications.

Planning

The account planner interprets the client's research as well as consumer trends to develop the creative brief and manage the work through the creative department, making sure that the work stays on strategy during its development.

Creative team/Producer

This traditionally consists of a copywriter (the person who writes the promotional copy) and an art director (the person who designs the ad). The creative team actually develops the ads or other marketing communications. While having a team of two became common during the 1960s, today we are returning to the time when a single person works as both copywriter and art director.

The producer takes the idea, script, layout and so on, and makes it into a final film or print advertisement (or whatever the medium).

← Distribution channel marketing
→ **Promotion in marketing**
→› Appendix

Internet specialist

Eventually, the Internet creative will probably fold into the overall creative group. However, given that Internet development and production is still relatively new and very different from development and production in older forms of media, this is still dealt with separately at this time.

Media

The media group determines the best place to put marketing communications to maximise their impact and negotiates the optimum price for the placement.

Public relations/event marketer

The public relations representative determines the most favourable way to manage the company's public image in the news.

Promotions/relationship marketing

The promotions representative determines the optimal short-term incentives to gain trial of the product as well as the best long-term way to build a strong customer relationship.

Developing a strategy

Strategy development is probably the most important single step in creating a successful brand. Your strategy is all about what you are going to tell your target audience to get them to do what you want them to do. The actual advert or marketing communication development is taking the 'what' information and defining 'how' you will present it.

Think of your strategy as a road map

Building a brand is similar to planning a complicated road trip. If you have no strategy, or if it's too vague a strategy, you'll wander the countryside never finding the place you want to go. If your strategy is precise and accurate, you manage all the twists and turns and arrive exactly where you want to be and, with a little luck, on time.

For example, let's assume that Toyota wants you as a customer from the first car you buy to the last car you own. If that's what they are aiming for – how do you get there (in other words, what is their strategy?). Toyota made the strategic decision to launch a line of quality, less expensive cars under the Scion badge. The cars are designed for a younger buyer and provide terrific value at a very reasonable price. But we all grow up and our families expand. Toyota has you covered with a full line of cars and trucks offering everything you might need for a young family or small business. And if you reach a point where you can afford a true luxury automobile, then Toyota has the Lexus line of cars providing the same reliable car in a very luxurious version. That's how Toyota can sell cars priced from $16,000 to over $100,000 and satisfy your every car need from your first to your last.

Your strategy is the road map that gets you from where you are to where you want to go.

←← The communications revolution
→ **Developing marketing communications**
→→ The creative process

151

Capable of things your courage isn't.

THE ALL-NEW 383-HORSEPOWER* LX 570.

This is the driver, empowered. When activated, an innovative off-road control feature, called Crawl Control,¹ allows you to physically take your feet off the pedals and concentrate on steering as your vehicle slowly negotiates the delicate exchange of gas and brake on sections of rough terrain.   *The pursuit of perfection*

DriverEmpowered.com

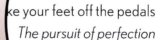

ke your feet off the pedals
The pursuit of perfection

152   **The Fundamentals of Marketing**

⤎ Distribution channel marketing
➜ **Promotion in marketing**
⇾ Appendix

Creative strategy

The creative strategy is the 'what' you plan to say about your brand that will trigger the result you are looking for. You will share this with your creative team who will use it as a road map for what must be communicated, and your creative team will figure out how best to communicate that information.

Let's use the Toyota Lexus as our example. Back in the 1980s, Toyota wanted to enter the luxury car market dominated by German manufacturers BMW and Mercedes. Toyota had built a reputation as a reliable, good value car, but certainly not a competitor to Mercedes. Toyota decided on a strategy that introduced a separate car line named Lexus sold at separate dealerships. Everyone knew Lexus was a product of Toyota so the reputation for reliability haloed the brand.

In the case of Lexus, Toyota understood that all Japanese products were gaining a reputation for reliability and flawless production. Additionally, German products focused more on performance and technology and weren't always 'perfect'. The creative team at Team One (a division of Saatchi & Saatchi) penned the line 'The pursuit of perfection' to not only set the Lexus apart as a clearly superior car to the Mercedes, but also to take advantage of Mercedes and BMW's occasional manufacturing flaws. In doing this, Lexus effectively redefined luxury as perfect production instead of stronger performance. Within about a decade, consumers had changed their expectations and Lexus became the largest manufacturer of luxury cars in the world.

Toyota's sales strategy of introducing a separate line under a separate name along with the decision to position these as perfect luxury cars, successfully unseated one of the strongest brands in the world.

Creative brief formats

Every company has their own particular creative strategy (or creative brief) format, but nearly all the information called for is the same wherever you work. The brief below is a compilation of some of the best in the business. There are eight questions you must answer:

1) What is the specific job of the advertising?
2) Who is our target?
3) What do they currently think?
4) What do we want them to think?
5) What is the single most compelling promise we can make?
6) How do we make it believable?
7) Is there anything else worth considering that may help us get great creative work?
8) Are there any 'executional mandatories'?

What is the specific job of the advertising?

What are you trying to accomplish in communications? What is your communications objective? Note that the word 'communications' is critical.

This objective is not to be stated as a sales or marketing objective (for example, to increase sales 5%). All advertising is (or should be) designed to increase sales so the use of a sales number is redundant. The objective should not be stated as a media objective either (such as to increase brand awareness). You could run a 30-second logo on television and accomplish an awareness increase.

A communication objective defines what must be communicated in order to get the prospect (or consumer) to do what you want them to do (for example, 'convince our potential target that Lexus is a perfect luxury car'). A good way to make sure you do this correctly is simply to start the sentence with the phrase 'Convince consumers that…'.

←← The communications revolution
→ **Developing marketing communications**
→→ The creative process

153

Who is our target?

The goal of the target section is to get your creative team to be able to say 'I know that person'. Far too many creative briefs are written with a media target like 'women between the ages of 18 and 49 years old'). Who is a woman between 18 and 49? Chances are this description would include over half of the students reading this book and their mothers. Are you and your mother exactly the same?

Creatives write much better ads if they feel as if they know their target personally. Which of the target descriptions below would you rather write a Lexus ad for?

Target description one: Wealthy men over 50 years old.

Target description two: Kevin appreciates the finer things in life like family, friends and a good education. He is Senior Vice President of Marketing for a major food company and just celebrated is 25th anniversary with his company. Both he and his wife have their Master of Business Administration. Kevin plays golf with friends and his wife is very involved in several local charities and arts organisations. Kevin has owned BMWs and Mercedes, but feels that they are too showy. He has nothing to prove; he just wants the best-built, most reliable car he can get.

What do they currently think?

It's important to understand what the target consumer currently thinks about the product category, the competitive brands in the category as well as what aspirations they may have for the future. Going back to the Lexus example for a moment, what does the Mercedes buyer think about all these things?

'I'm a car fanatic and I've been a loyal Mercedes buyer for years. I like the quality and prestige of driving the best car in the world. However, my current Mercedes has more mechanical issues than ever. They just don't seem as good as they used to be. I've even heard on the news that Mercedes reliability was ranked last in *Consumer Reports*. That's worrying.'

As a creative, I can begin to understand this potential customer's motivations (quality and prestige), their level of loyalty ('they just don't seem to be as good as they used to be') and even their potential vulnerability (reliability issues). If I can understand their mindset, I have a much better chance of changing their buying habits.

What do we want them to think?

We know what they think, but what would we like them to think in order for them to do what we want? Again, back to the Lexus example: we want them to think that Lexus makes the best quality car in the world, not Mercedes.

Do you think that if your target really considered Lexus a better-quality car than Mercedes then they would change their purchase behaviour? If it carried enough prestige, they certainly would.

154 |**The Fundamentals of Marketing**

←← Distribution channel marketing
→ **Promotion in marketing**
→→ Appendix

What is the single most compelling promise we can make?

Now, we know who these people are, we know what they think, we know what we want them to think. What is the single most compelling promise we can make to these people to move them from point A to point B?

Let's consider a few different types of claims we can make using our Lexus example:

→ **The unique selling proposition:** The new Lexus is the most reliable luxury car you can buy.
  → This is an overt statement of superiority, or something unique that no one else could say.
→ **Positioning claim:** The new Lexus is the highest-quality luxury car you can buy.
  → This is a statement that positions your product in comparison to brands the consumer already knows.
→ **Generic superiority:** No one makes a better luxury car than Lexus.
  → Note, they could all be equally as good and this statement would still be legal.
→ **Pre-emptive claim:** Every Lexus goes through a 210-point quality control test.
  → Note that possibly every car made does this, however, if no other manufacturer is saying it; Lexus 'owns' the statement.
→ **Brand image:** Driving the new Lexus tells people you care more about quality than show.
  → Lexus is all about the quality of the car and will let other manufacturers have style without substance.
→ **Resonance claim:** It is no coincidence that the traditional 25th anniversary gift is a new Lexus.
  → Attaching your brand to fundamental human experiences such as love, marriage or patriotism can help the brand resonate with your consumer.

How do we make it believable?

Consumers have learned not to trust advertising. Annual research ranking careers on their level of ethics consistently ranks advertising practitioners at number two – from the very bottom. Only used-car dealers are viewed as less ethical than advertising practitioners. Therefore, how do you make your claim believable? Use indisputable or provable facts.

→ **Proposition:** 'The new Lexus is the most reliable luxury car you can buy.'

→ **How do we make it believable?** 'The new Lexus is the top-ranked luxury auto in initial quality by JD Powers and associates for the last ten years running.'

→ **Translation:** 'We're the best because actual owners say we are and say our competition isn't.'

> **We started out to be the best. We never imagined we would be the biggest. Lexus is about providing our customers the best possible experience. One that we know will keep getting better and better.**
> Bob Carter

←← The communications revolution
→ **Developing marketing communications**
→→ The creative process

155

Is there anything else worth considering that may help us get great creative work?

It's important to understand two very important things when finding a creative team to work on your project:

1) Only about 20% of the creatives in a big agency are really talented (creatives, don't be insulted, it's about the same for every position).

2) Good creatives have about five different brands to create ads for at the same time as your ad. In other words, you want to attract the very best talent in the company to want to work on your ad, and you want to give them an incentive that says your business is better than all the others on their plate.

Is there anything else worth considering that may help us get great creative work? Is auto advertising a particularly award-winning category in advertising award shows? Does Lexus buy award-winning work? Do you have a commitment for a large budget behind the ad? Is this a growing account? There are hundreds of scenarios that will get you the extra attention you want from the most talented people.

Are there any executional mandatories?

Executional mandatories are elements that you are required to use in the ad. For example, if Lexus is using the 'Relentless pursuit of perfection' selling line, they may (and should) require you to use it in every advert. Other mandatories usually include web addresses, logos, legal copy and copyright logos. If you have none, leave it blank.

Common variations of this strategy format

As we said, every agency has their own format, but truth be told they are all very similar. Some common variations include the following.

Positioning statement

Sometimes brands will insist that the positioning statement is included on every brief. This is a perfectly fine idea as it's not uncommon to have different creative groups produce each promotion and consistency in advertising will help your funds go further.

Consumer insight

A consumer insight is knowledge of a particular aspect of human behaviour that can connect your consumer to your brand. For example, there is nothing a new father wouldn't do (even putting his own life in jeopardy) to protect his newborn child.

Competition

The brief should make it clear who the most direct competition will be for the product, although it might not be mentioned overtly.

Brand essence

A brand essence statement is usually one or two words that sum up what the brand means to consumers. The essence of McDonald's for children is 'fun'. The essence of American Express is 'security'. The essence of the Hummer brand is 'conquest to domination'. By summarising the brand in a short phrase, everyone working on the brand can use this as a guiding principle to make sure they manage the brand and brand reputation correctly.

156 **The Fundamentals of Marketing**

←← Distribution channel marketing
➜ **Promotion in marketing**
⇢ Appendix

Tone of voice

Do you work for a serious brand? A humorous brand? A desperate brand? Chances are your communications have a certain tonality and it will be your responsibility to match that tone. A humorous Microsoft ad just wouldn't seem right: Microsoft is visionary. A hard-sell Lexus ad wouldn't seem right. A humorous ad from the Red Cross might make you think that blood donation is not all that important.

Strategy and execution

Once you have determined what you need to say in order to get your target to do what you want them to do, it's time to figure out where you should put your message before you concentrate on how to say it.

Selecting media (media plan)

Should you advertise on TV, the Internet, in magazine ads or as a label on oranges in a supermarket? The answer might be all of these or none of these. Media planners are experts in figuring out not only where you should advertise, but when. It's critical that the media group get the opportunity to figure out where and when to advertise before the creative team goes off to create ads.

The key to using media as a strategy for your brand is to maintain 100% media neutrality. 'Media neutrality' means that no certain media are preferred over another at the beginning of the process. You agree your target will define what media your promotions should appear in, as well as when, where and how. That sounds like simple common sense, but marketers and agencies become so entrenched in 'how we've done it before', methods that have proven successful and what the creative team wants to produce, that it's rare that we get a truly media-neutral campaign.

How do we reach true media neutrality? It's really relatively simple. We have quantitative research (MRI & Simmons Research) showing which media is used by a particular audience at a particular time and place. We also have a simple little exercise called 'Day in the life' where we track our target from the time they wake up until the time they go back to bed and follow every step they take during the day. 'Day in the life' is meant to track their movements as well as pinpoint potential media they are exposed to each moment of the day.

There is also research available that will rank media to help determine when your target will be most interested in the particular message you have to deliver. For example, if you want to sell life insurance, you are basically wasting your time and money to try to attract single people ('why would I want to leave money to anyone?') or newly married couples ('hey, he/she is young and healthy, let them get a job!'), but try selling life insurance to a couple with a newborn and you have someone that wants your product and wants it now.

← The communications revolution
→ **Developing marketing communications**
→→ The creative process

157

The creative process

At this point you know what to say (your creative brief) and where you need to say it (your media plan). Now it's time to figure out how to deliver the message by creating the ads and other individual pieces of communication.

To figure out this 'how' element of the process, the full team would traditionally get together to discuss the creative brief and timing of the project. Creative teams would then go away to brainstorm lots of different solutions. They would take what they thought were their best ideas to their creative director who would choose three, present them internally and prepare to present them to the client. In the client meeting, the agency would present three campaign directions, recommend one and negotiate an outcome with their client. Most large agencies still work under this model.

However, some agencies will put everyone working on a project in one room with a professional moderator and have them brainstorm as many ideas as possible. Everyone contributes and often the client is included. The advantage of the one-room model is that more people contribute and own the ideas and generally there is a greater diversity of ideas. Once the team agrees which concepts should be pursued, the creative team executes the ideas.

Alternatively, there is the 'global brainstorm' model which brings senior creatives from around the world together to develop a campaign for a major global brand available in their country. Given the same brief, you are likely to get very different solutions from your Australian creative director than from your German one, your American one and so on. In the end, your client will have a great diversity of thought to select from.

Who should be in charge?

Who determines what types of communications will be pursued and which will be shelved? If anyone from the advertising agency is in charge of creative development, how can the solution NOT be advertising-centric? No one in today's ad agency is thoroughly trained outside the advertising discipline. The same is true of the other disciplines. Even if you do train advertising people to thoroughly understand PR, sales promotion and so on it's still an advertising agency writing their pay cheque.

One seemingly obvious conclusion is that marketers should take on this responsibility. Maybe that's true, but MBA programmes teach almost nothing about communications and brand managers don't do enough of it to build any real expertise.

158   **The Fundamentals of Marketing**

←← Distribution channel marketing
➜ **Promotion in marketing**
⟶⟩ Appendix

Media planning and buying companies could be in charge, and some are taking that role. However, most of them do not hold the expertise in disciplines outside advertising, making discipline-neutral planning unlikely.

Enter Naked. Naked is a London-based communications planning firm made up largely of ex-media planners and account planners. They only plan. They do not make ads, nor are they attached to any company that does. While only a short time ago this might have seemed a niche idea, Naked works with some of the world's largest and most powerful marketers such as Johnson & Johnson from the US.

Entering the black box

Creatives often refer to creative development as 'entering the black box' where ideas mysteriously jumble around until the muse gives birth to that stroke of genius. The actual creation is truly a combination of perspiration and inspiration. Writers will write literally hundreds of headlines trying to free their minds to go into new areas.

The most valuable portion of communication is known as the 'big idea'. A big idea is an idea that can serve as a company's rallying cry and permeate every part of what the company stands for. 'The pursuit of perfection' tells designers how to design a Lexus, the mechanic how to fix a Lexus, the car dealer how to sell and deliver a Lexus and the owner what to expect of Lexus.

Fig. 6-5: James Webb Young's technique for producing ideas
Back in the 1920s, ad-man James Webb Young sought to figure out how he and others developed advertising ideas. This five-step process hasn't really changed in the ensuing 90 years.

Step 1: Immersion
Immerse yourself in everything you can possibly learn about your product, your competition, your target audience and so on.

1

Step 2: Digestion
Digest all this information to figure out what is most important and most helpful.

2

Step 3: Incubation
Drop all thought of the project. Go to the movies, play video games, read a good book. Your subconscious will juggle the information on its own, giving birth to idea after idea.

3

Step 4: Illumination
Eureka! Well formed ideas will begin flowing. Allow your brain to kick out as many as you can. Write them down and keep going. When they appear to be slowing significantly, only then should you begin to judge and determine which you believe is the best idea to work on.

4

Step 5: Reality testing
Will it really work? Run your idea by people you respect and who will tell you the truth. Some of the ideas I've developed over time that I thought were absolutely fantastic were simply un-doable. Others were simply confusing. Reality testing will keep you on the straight and narrow.

5

←← Developing marketing communications
→ **The creative process**
→→→ Pitching the concept

159

Developing the communications

Beyond how creative people actually develop and judge ideas, there is a process that takes you from 'I need an ad' to the finished advertisement appearing on television. This process can take anywhere from a day to more than 40 weeks, depending on the level of difficulty of the commercial and the level of risk you are willing to assume.

The basics of the process are the same no matter what medium you choose:
1) Agree what is needed (objective)
2) Agree what the communication should say (strategy)
3) Develop the ad
4) Make the idea into an actual advert ready to run in the media.

While that sounds simple, for a television commercial the process can easily involve over 100 people and, start to finish, it can take as long as it takes to have a baby.

Print ads (newspaper and magazine) are much faster, but still involve hiring actors/models and photographers and can easily take eight to ten weeks. Outdoor advertisements are developed in a similar way to print ads but require large-scale printing and posting that can lengthen production time and require hiring outside facilities. Radio ads are one of the simplest and fastest to produce while online advertisements can be developed in a matter of hours depending on the talent of your programmers.

Advertising production is among the most detailed and stringent of any type of production. Ads must fit exactly into a 15- or 30-second break and when you are trying to tell a very complicated story in 30 seconds, every shot has to be perfect. It's not unusual in a TV commercial to shoot a five-second scene more than 50 times to get every detail and inflection absolutely perfect. TV celebrities who agree to do commercials are quite often shocked by the level of perfection demanded.

The 40-week chart

Let's take an in-depth look at the creation of a television commercial from 'I need an ad' to seeing the finished commercial on air. Note how many steps and how many different people take control at different parts of the process. Also note that clients with a lot of money at risk tend to want proof the ad is going to work before it goes on air.

40-week chart
There certainly isn't one right way to develop and produce a television commercial, but the process outlined here will show the most formal and careful version. Anything less than this basically requires cutting steps or cutting time in the process.

160 |The Fundamentals of Marketing

←← Distribution channel marketing
➔ **Promotion in marketing**
→→ Appendix

Step in the process	Everyone involved	Who is in charge?	Time
'We need an ad' Client recognises need for new TV commercial.	Client, Account Management	Client	1 day
Briefing meeting Agency puts together core team that will work on a project beginning to end. Client presents all relevant research.	Client, Account Management, Planning, Creative, Media	Client/Account Management	1 day
Creative brief development Planner develops creative brief sharing with other members of the team prior to client presentation.	Account Management, Planning, Creative, Media	Planning	1 week
Creative brief presentation Brief presented to client for input/approval.	Client, Account Management, Planning, Creative, Media	Planning	1 day
Creative brief revisions Assuming the client has some requested changes.	Planning, Client, Account Management	Planning	1 week
Creative brief testing If the brief reflects a new direction for the brand, chances are the client will want to test the strategy prior to creative development.	Planning, Account Management	Planning	1 week
Final creative brief approval	Client, Account Management, Planning, Creative, Media	Planning	1 day
First look Agency team will look at and comment on the first round of ideas for a commercial with the Creative Director, choosing 3–5 directions to concentrate on.	Account Management, Planning, Creative	Creative Director	2–3 weeks
Final concepts Agency develops the 3–5 directions in all required media (assuming the media plan calls for more than TV).	Account Management, Planning, Creative, Media	Creative Director	1 week
Pre-testing concepts If the ideas seem too controversial or esoteric, Planning may choose to pre-test to make sure they are presenting clear and compelling concepts.	Account Management, Planning	Planning	2–3 days

←← Developing marketing communications
➜ **The creative process**
⟶⟩ Pitching the concept

161

Step in the process	Everyone involved	Who is in charge?	Time
Internal presentation This is essentially a rehearsal for the client presentation.	Account Management, Planning, Creative, Media	Creative Director	1 day
Client presentation Agency presents 3–5 campaign ideas and recommends the one they believe is best.	Client, Account Management, Planning, Creative, Media	Account Management	3 days
Revised concepts Client has expressed a preference for an ad and likely asked for some changes. Agency executes changes and re-presents new work.	Client, Account Management, Planning, Creative, Media	Account Management, Client	1 week
Animatic testing Client likely wants quantitative evidence the commercial will work so they produce some inexpensive version of the commercial for testing prior to spending the budget on the final production.	Planning, Creative, Account Management	Planning Production	3 weeks Testing 6 weeks
Research results discussion Planning presents the results of the testing	Client, Account Management, Planning, Creative	Planning	1 day
Revised creative concepts Agency learns from research and may make changes to the TV storyboard to make the concept clearer, more competitive, more effective.	Client, Account Management, Planning, Creative	Creative Director	1 week
Pre-bid meeting Core team has final approved TV storyboard and research evidence it will work. Now it's time to move toward final production.	Client, Account Management, Creative, Production	Producer	1 week
Director selection The agency producer presents around 12 commercial reels from potential directors/production companies. Along with the art director and copywriter, they agree the best three directors to shoot the commercial and secure bids from those three.	Client, Account Management, Creative, Production	Producer, Creative Team	1-2 weeks
Bid meeting Meeting with client to agree how bidding will proceed. Agency presents two to three directors / production companies for approval.	Client, Account Management, Creative, Production	Producer	1 day

Step in the process	Everyone involved	Who is in charge?	Time
Bid approval Directors have submitted production cost bids, Client/Agency have approved a bid and awarded the job.	Client, Account Management, Creative, Production	Production	3 weeks
Pre-production meeting Single meeting where every detail of a production is agreed prior to the production of a commercial. This includes casting, wardrobe, sets, locations and so on.	Client, Account Management, Creative, Production, Director	Producer/Director	3 weeks
TV production Commercial prepped and shot.	Client, Account Management, Creative, Production, Director	Director	2 weeks prep 2–3 days shoot
Rough cut presentation A rough cut is the first cut of a commercial without any scene transitions, music, sound effects and so on.	Director, Producer, Creative Team	Producer	1–2 weeks
Revised rough cut presentation Chances are the client had some comments and a revision was necessary	Client, Account Management, Planning, Creative Team, Producer	Producer	1 week
Finished film presentation Final film completed with all video and audio transitions complete.	Client, Account Management, Planning, Creative Director, Creative Team, Producer	Producer	2 weeks
Potentially more communications research Many large clients require that all finished commercials are quantitatively tested prior to air.	Client, Account Management, Planning	Planning	6–8 weeks
Final approval to air All testing complete, this meeting is a final approval often including client senior management to get all final approvals prior to air.	Client, Account Management, Planning, Creative Director, Creative Team, Producer	Account Management	1 day
Traffic Commercial Commercial sent to TV station.	Account Management, Media, Agency Traffic Department	Traffic Department, Media	3 weeks
Commercial on air	Media	Media	Done!
30 steps			**40+ weeks**

← Developing marketing communications
→ **The creative process**
→→ Pitching the concept

163

Pitching the concept

I worked with a creative director for many years who used to tell her teams 'the very best advertising ideas in the world, unsold, are known as landfill'. It's sad, but true. The presentation and selling of the ideas is as critical as the idea itself.

Most presentations consist of the same seven steps:
1) Discussion of the assignment
2) Presentation of the creative brief
3) Presentation of the creative idea
4) Presentation of the creative possibilities
5) Recommendation of a single idea
6) Selling of the idea
7) Discussion/agreement to next steps

There's nothing inherently wrong with this meeting format, but that's just it – it can begin to feel like a format.

A former client once told my agency that we were the most fun time of his day. I began by feeling sorry for him, until I realised that it was our responsibility to make each meeting as engaging and enjoyable as possible. That led us to adding a lot of fun and excitement to our meetings as we took this responsibility more seriously. We acted out commercials, presented our work in the environment it would be shown, and did whatever we could to make approving our recommendation as enjoyable and painless as possible.

Put yourself in the client's chair

This is an important meeting. Your client may have enough money to take one shot at making their brand successful. If the communications fail, their career may fail. In an agency, if the commercial fails, you go and write something for someone else.

It should be a positive buying experience. Any good client comes to a meeting hoping to see a solution to their communications problem. They are on your side and desperately want you to succeed. Think about buying experiences you've had (such as buying a car or laptop computer). You can learn a lot from both your good experiences and bad experiences being on the other side of the table.

Find a very engaging way to begin your meeting

You have about 90 seconds to engage your audience before you risk losing their interest for the entire meeting. If you engage your audience from the very beginning, you are far more likely to make the sale. For example, people love good stories with a beginning, middle and end. Turn your presentation into a captivating story with only one potential outcome: a sale.

164 | **The Fundamentals of Marketing**

⇐ Distribution channel marketing
➜ **Promotion in marketing**
⟶ Appendix

Have only the best presenters present

The cost of not making a sale is simply too high in time and money. In the real world, only the best presenters should present – so make sure you are one of them. Also, assign one person to listen to the dress rehearsal of your meeting and cut away every piece of information that doesn't get you to the conclusion you want. You are not presenting – you are selling.

Know the room

Technical problems in a room can ruin a presentation. Know your room ahead of time and make no assumptions about the capabilities of the room (this is especially true as most agency people work on Macintosh computers while most marketers work on PCs).

It's a sin to bore a client

You want your client to produce and air engaging advertising, so why would your presentation be any less engaging?

Avoid overused presentation formats. Are you getting tired of seeing PowerPoint? So is your client. Try different formats and keep each meeting new and different. Use good visuals; they are far more memorable.

Make contact with everyone in the room, but sell to the decision maker(s). I once spent nearly an hour presenting/selling to what I thought was the most senior person in the room and, I believed, the decision maker. He was with me all the way nodding and laughing at exactly the right point. I was very proud of myself and my presentation – until I found out he was the CEO's chauffeur.

Let your client talk

I was once told by a colleague that I have a tendency to talk too much in meetings. Being an extreme type, I decided to not talk at all in the next new business pitch. I asked four questions and allowed the potential client to talk as much as they wanted to. I was very responsive visually, but said nothing. Another member of the team overheard the CEO telling his marketing manager after leaving our nearly three-hour meeting that he thought I was far and away the most intelligent managing director of an advertising agency he had met. They awarded us the business without a formal pitch. And I learned a valuable lesson. People love to talk – let them.

Be prepared for questions

Anticipate your audience's questions and be prepared with who on your team will answer and how they will answer. DO NOT talk over each other, or repeat answers others have given.

Be honest

If something is going wrong, admit it. If you don't have the answer to a question, say so (then go get it). Clients don't expect you to have all the answers all the time, but they do know when they are being lied to and they won't put up with it.

←← The creative process
➜ **Pitching the concept**
→→ Assessing marketing communications

165

Assessing marketing communications

There is little in life more intimidating than being presented with 'new to the world' ideas and being asked to comment on them. While it may seem simple, answers such as: 'I like it, it's cool' won't make it in the real world. So, how should you think about new ads? Firstly, it is important to ask whether the suggested new advert is on-strategy. You've all agreed the strategy is correct; does the new ad fit that strategy? Once you determine that the ad is on-strategy, then your personal opinion of what you like and don't like may be relevant.

Next, ask whether the ad will appeal to the right audience? Your personal opinion of the ad is really only relevant if you represent the entire target audience. I once produced what I thought would be the best campaign of my career. It was very exciting. When the ads ran, current users of the product (our target audience) actually stopped using the product. My opinion wasn't really relevant. Had I asked what the target would think I might not have made such a huge mistake.

Finally, you must run through the three 'C's'. Is the advert clear, concise and convincing? Will the target market understand what you are trying to communicate? People like being intrigued by advertising, but won't spend their afternoon trying to figure out what you are trying to say about the product. Once they've understood the message, they also need to clearly understand what you want them to do.

What if your ad is off-strategy and better than the strategy?

It happens. You work hard on a strategy and the creative team comes through with something that is clearly off-strategy, but a better idea than the strategy. What do you do? Answer: have the courage of your convictions to admit that the creative team had a better idea than the strategists did and rewrite the strategy if it's truly better. But, be honest with everyone about what you are doing and why.

166   **The Fundamentals of Marketing**

←← Distribution channel marketing
→ **Promotion in marketing**
→→ Appendix

Researching communications

Creative people (in general) hate testing their work. It's difficult enough to develop new ideas and can be quite humiliating to have laymen tell you they don't understand them. But research is a fact of marketing life and you'll be better off getting good at it than just whining about its existence. In general, the earlier you research in the process (for example, research the strategy) the better for everyone.

Researching the strategy/brief

Researching the strength and clarity of the brief can help produce better work. This is often done in the form of a concept statement and put into a competitive ranking to make sure you have the strongest possible strategy to build from.

Researching the communications

Research isn't bad; it's the interpretation of the research that can be bad. Research can be very helpful in making even great ideas better. The problem is in how the research is understood, interpreted and followed. Those who follow every word that comes out of a consumer's mouth often end up with mediocrity. Consumers have trouble reacting to ideas they've never seen before and tend to push to get back into familiar areas they are more comfortable discussing. If you understand that prior to the research, you can interpret what is said in a way that will actually allow you to strengthen an idea, not dilute it. What do we test for? Persuasion, salience, recall, messages communicated and clarity. If we can strengthen these areas, why wouldn't we?

Advertising research exists because, used correctly, it can help avoid costly mistakes and make successes even larger. Used incorrectly, it can kill great ideas and guarantee mediocrity in sales as well.

Good ad? Bad ad?
With the tag line 'It's all the same to us', students at Syracuse University found a visual way to tell a product story about Pledge Multi-Surface Cleaner. This advert won the Lürzer's Archive International Student of the Year contest (2007) and was published in ARCHIVE, the leading international magazine dedicated to advertising creativity.

← Pitching the concept
→ Assessing marketing communications
→→ Measuring effectiveness

167

Ethical dilemmas

This chart describes some of the ethical dilemmas advertisers get themselves into and how most marketers and advertising agencies handle them. Personal ethical standards are just that: personal. I doubt many would advocate knowingly breaking the law, but beyond that, decisions can become very grey. How you handle these ethical dilemmas is a matter of personal choice and defines who you are as a person.

Ethical dilemma

Harmful products: Should we be allowed to sell products that are clearly harmful to the health of the user? Cigarettes are an obvious ethical dilemma, but from there it's not difficult to get to alcohol (drunk driving), fats (obesity and heart disease), guns (gun violence) and so on.

Content regulation and censorship: Should advertising dollars be supporting the production and airing of shows that promote racism, sexism or may incite violence?

Big agency/client response

While products such as cigarettes are clearly dangerous, they are legal. In most countries, manufacturers of legal products have the right to promote them in some way.

Advertisers tend not to want to associate themselves with controversy. They like big audiences, but prefer avoiding excessive violence, racism or sexism. Most major advertisers actually have advertising guidelines and even a small department that view shows prior to air to decide whether or not to advertise on a particular show.

Don Imus, a very popular radio personality in the US, was fired in 2007 – not for the racist and sexist remarks he made on the air about the Rutgers University women's basketball team, but because over a week after the controversy began, his advertisers pulled their ads. Only the prospect of losing advertising revenue was strong enough motivation to persuade the management of CBS radio to fire Imus.

This isn't a role advertising agencies are particularly comfortable with, but it is their job to protect their clients from unwanted associations.

←← Distribution channel marketing
➜ **Promotion in marketing**
→→ Appendix

Ethical dilemma	Big agency/ Big client response
Advertising to children: Hundreds of studies from all around the globe have documented issues related to advertising to children. This has prompted regulations on advertising to children in Europe, parts of Asia and various markets in South America. The US has very few regulations.	Advertising and marketing personnel prefer self-regulation wherever possible and have set up organisations such as the Children's Advertising Review Unit (CARU) to review and make recommendations to individual advertisers. Every large advertising agency has a separate agency purely focused on promoting goods and services to children.
Globalisation: No matter what you think of globalisation, it would be difficult to argue that it didn't strip Western nations of their manufacturing base and lead to massive loss of jobs in these countries.	Most advertising agencies and marketers benefited greatly from globalising their own business and believe the trend was going to happen no matter what they did. And they are probably correct.
Advertising and obesity: Clearly the US, UK and many Western countries are experiencing obesity epidemics. Should advertising promote products that hold little nutritional value?	Like the issue with cigarettes, if the product is legal for sale, advertising agencies tend to believe we should be allowed to promote it.
Advertising and body image: Does advertising help create unrealistic versions of beauty in our society that can lead to unhealthy eating habits and eating disorders?	Yes, and we'll stop when the general culture stops responding positively to images of very slim young women. It's not advertising's job to shape culture, it's advertising's job to present products in their best possible light in order to make a sale.
Deceptive claims: The real reason ads say things like 'no toothpaste does a better job' is because the product's performance is in parity with its competitors but consumers hear 'this toothpaste does a better job'. Isn't that deceptive and shouldn't that be illegal?	It is deceptive when you know your customers are hearing something in a different context from the way you are saying it. But it's not illegal, and if it were, someone would find an even sneakier way to say it.

←← Pitching the concept
→ **Assessing marketing communications**
→→ Measuring effectiveness

169

Measuring effectiveness

So, you're ready to write your first marketing plan. But will it work? How will you know if it has worked? How will you make sure it works, before you execute it? That's right, it's not enough to monitor the success of the programme. If you aren't successful, you will have spent all your investment and have nothing to show for it. Today, you need to prove you are right each step along the way.

There are literally hundreds of ways to measure your success. The simplest and most used is to measure your progress against the objectives you have set up (or the business vision if you wrote one). Your management will want to make sure you have removed as much risk as possible and that means proving everything works, before you actually do it.

Current financial measures of success
You've probably heard of some of the financial measures we use to determine our level of success. Remember, in business, ultimately it's all about the money. Let's take a quick look at some of the more common financial measures of success.

→ ROI (return on investment): How much money have we made on our investment?
→ Revenue growth: How much did sales revenue grow either as a percentage or in currency?
→ Profit growth: Ultimately profit is the most important number, so did we grow overall profit or profit per item sold?
→ Growth of the market: Did we grow the entire category of goods to make it larger for ourselves and our competition?
→ Market share growth: What percentage of category sales do we have? That's our market share.
→ Dollar share: What percentage of category dollar sales do we have?
→ Unit share: What percentage of unit sales in the category do we have?
→ Demand growth: Have we actually increased demand for the product category or our brand?
→ Market penetration growth: Have we increased the number and percentage of people who are actually using the brand?
→ Customer profitability: Have we increased the profitability per customer either by increasing the profit per item sold, lowering the cost of each item sold or trading our customers up to more expensive or more profitable items?
→ Corporate earnings: Are we making more sales than we used to?
→ Marketing cost per unit: Have we increased or decreased the amount we spend in marketing for every unit sold?

170   **The Fundamentals of Marketing**

←← Distribution channel marketing
→ **Promotion in marketing**
→→ Appendix

Current brand-health measures of success

While money always remains critically important in business, brands can be measured in other ways to make sure that you are improving the health of the brand and not simply making more money. You will probably want to measure your success against both financial goals and brand-health goals.

→ Customer acquisition: Have we acquired more customers?
→ Customer retention: Customers tend to come and go. Have we kept a higher percentage of them than our competitors?
→ Share of requirements: Consumers tend to have several brands in any category that are perfectly fine substitutes for each other. Does our brand supply the requirements of our customers better than our competitors?
→ Trial: What percentage of our target audience have tried our brand?
→ Adoption: What percentage of consumers who try our brand are staying with us and making it their brand?
→ Usage: Do we have more day-to-day users than our competitors?
→ Purchase frequency: Are our customers buying the product more frequently?
→ Brand equity measures: Brand equity refers to those intangible descriptions that 'belong' to the brand. Are these measures increasing, decreasing or staying the same?
→ Preference: We want to always be the preferred brand among our target audience. Are we?
→ Recall and 'top of mind' awareness: What percentage of our target recall our brand or our advertising both unaided (without help) or aided (with help)?

Proving the marketing plan works

Before you get a chance to execute any part of your plan, you are going to need to prove that it works with your target audience. Every decision you've made needs validation to make sure that what you intend to come through is actually what is coming through from product to price to place to promotion.

Product testing/evaluation

Every aspect of your product will be tested. Generally you would have been giving free prototypes to consumers so they can use the product as they would in their normal lives. From this you'll get feedback on what they love, what they hate, as well as suggestions for how to make every aspect better. Be careful. Even the most creative respondent can drive you to mediocrity so avoid knee-jerk responses to everything they say. Take the smart ideas and avoid the dumb ones. You'll hear both.

Pricing

There is a right price for everything; you just need to find it. Price testing is best done with people with experience using your brand as they will know it better than anyone.

Distribution measures

Remember 'all commodity volume' from Chapter 5 (page 130)? ACV tells you whether or not the distribution you have built up will be adequate to build a strong brand. You may also want to test alternative distribution channels.

Marketing communications testing

How do we measure success? Sales? Profit? Passionate consumers? There are hundreds of ways to measure and quantify your success. The key is to determine how you plan to measure success before your marketing programme even begins.

→ Advertising to sales ratio: Some companies create a ratio of sales revenues divided by advertising expenditures. The higher that ratio the more efficient the advertising, the lower the ratio the less efficient the campaign was.
→ Strategic evaluation: Researching your strategy ahead of time (whether it be creative strategy, pricing strategy or distribution strategy, it is called strategic evaluation).
→ Message evaluation: Did your message actually communicate what you wanted it to? You may be surprised how often they don't!
→ Media evaluation: Are you using the most efficient media?
→ Campaign cohesiveness: All the different parts of a campaign should be communicating a single message. Do they?

Media evaluation

GRP: A gross rating point is a measurement of media weight. You weigh yourself in kilos or pounds, media gets measured in GRPs. GRPs are calculated by measuring the percentage you reach by the number of times in a four-week period that you reach them. For example, if you reach 80% of your target audience four times over a four-week period, you simply multiply the two of them and you have 320 GRPs. Now you can compare the media weight of one plan against another or one year's media plan against another.

CPP: 'Cost per point' or CPP allows you to compare the efficiency between different media plans. Simply divide your media cost by the number of total GRPs and you have your cost per point.

Direct mail/Direct response: Marketers tend to be very numbers-driven people and they love when they can get facts of response to advertising. Direct marketing actually asks for an order and so it is easy to get response rates. In the case of direct mail 2–3% is about the average response rate you should expect.

Internet measurements

The Internet is a direct-response medium where you can find out how many people have seen your site (hits) or how many have reacted to either an ad or a website and clicked through to a deeper page. Again, this is measurable, unlike most media choices.

Search marketing: There are approximately 200 million individual websites on the Internet. Search marketing has become extremely important if you want to be seen. Search marketing involves paying search engines such as Google a fee to add your brand in the column on the right when certain search words are input. This is Google's main source of revenue.

Test marketing

By the time you've arrived at a full-blown marketing plan you should have tested each step along the way. So now you are ready to go national with your plan, correct? Usually not. When you take your marketing plan across the country, it's very expensive. For example, if you introduced the Smart Battery in the US, you'd need to invest at least $20 million in media. You know everything works separately, but you don't know if it all works well together. You only get one opportunity to introduce it nationally. Many marketers will try one more step, which is to put the product into test market for a period of time (usually a year).

A test market is a representative city or group of shops with isolated media where you can run your entire marketing programme as you plan to nationally. You can measure your success and both improve your marketing plan and get good quantitative evidence to help you predict how much product you will probably sell nationally.

The good side of test marketing:
→ You get the opportunity to test ideas before going national.
→ You can improve your plan before going national.
→ You risk little by comparison.

The bad side of test marketing:
→ Your competition will know exactly what you are planning to do and could even beat you to market.

172   **The Fundamentals of Marketing**

←← Distribution channel marketing
→ **Promotion in marketing**
→→ Appendix

Campaign for real beauty

When Unilever decided that the Dove brand should stand for a point of view rather a functional claim, the Dove Campaign for Real Beauty was born. If you are unfamiliar with the campaign, I encourage you to check out the website <www.campaignforrealbeauty.com> and take a look at their commercials Evolution and Onslaught available on YouTube.

Dove started the Campaign for Real Beauty in 2004 and since then has won a Grand Effie from the American Marketing Association (the top award for successful marketing efforts), the Grand Prix at the Cannes International Advertising Festival (the top advertising award in the world) and showed the world a brand can have a conscience. However, more importantly for Unilever, the campaign (along with a major brand expansion into some new categories) also increased brand sales by more than $1.2 billion worldwide.

While without question, the Campaign for Real Beauty has been a huge success at least in the short term, it hasn't been without controversy. Some have complained that these 'real women' all still have perfect skin, perfectly straight and white teeth and the largest woman used in the campaign is actually the same

size as the average American woman. So what's the bottom line? A marketing person's job is to build their business, not to make social statements, cure cultural issues or make us feel better about ourselves. With the help of a very smart promotional plan and great work by their ad agency Ogilvy & Mather and PR firm Edelman Public Relations, they really built their business.

Case study: Red Bull

In much of Asia, energy tonics are sold in pharmacies. These energy tonics sell for very little money and are primarily used by factory workers needing a boost to work a second shift. There is nothing glamorous about them; they are just a way of life. Enter Dietrich Mateschitz…

Dietrich Mateschitz
Dietrich Mateschitz was an Austrian-born salesman for Procter & Gamble working in Thailand. Mateschitz sold toothpaste to pharmacies in Thailand. Seeing people buying these small bottles of tonic day after day piqued his interest and so he took one called *Krating Daeng* (Thai for Red Bull) home in 1982. Upon realising that *Krating Daeng* was pretty much a 'cure' for jet lag, he started thinking about how he might be able to sell these throughout Europe and the rest of the world. In 1984, Mateschitz contracted with TC Pharmaceutical (maker of Krating Daeng) to form the Red Bull Beverage Company. After reformulating Krating Daeng with lightly carbonated water and a few other minor changes to better suit the European palate, Red Bull was introduced in 1987 and the new category of energy drinks, or functional beverages, was born.

The problem with introducing a new soft drink is that soft drink giants such as Coca-Cola and Pepsi-Cola are particularly interested in giving up shelf space and retailers expect tremendous turnover for a product to get distribution in the first place. So how get a new brand started?

In the case of Red Bull, you do it someplace a bit more open to innovation and a place not dominated by only a few very powerful marketers: bars. Red Bull started selling in bars, mostly individually owned and very interested in a product that sells as a mixer at $2 a can minimum. Once the club-culture of Europe adopted Red Bull as a staple product to be used for all-night clubbing, retail distributors had little choice but to force a slower selling/less profitable product to the side and replace it with Red Bull.

Bars were a great way to begin to build distribution, but more fundamentally, how do you build awareness when you have little money to spend on expensive advertising campaigns? Red Bull has become a major success story for guerrilla marketing. This includes events like *Flugtag* (Flight Day) where people compete by creating flying machines made of bathtubs and just about anything else guaranteed not to fly and then sailing them off islands in the Danube in Vienna, or piers off the Hudson River in New York, or any of about 50 other locations around the world. These have become annual events that draw huge television audiences year after year.

But *Flugtag* was only the beginning. As the brand grew, they began to sponsor extreme sports and extreme athletes. Suddenly you had people sailing off skyscrapers, monuments, a fleet of fighter jets, aerobatic trick planes and just about anything that flew had a Red Bull logo attached.

Their brilliant 'anti-advertising-advertising' as created by Johannes Kastner of Kastner & Partners undersells the product to a young hip and sceptical audience that hates advertising but adores Red Bull. Red Bull gives you wings. Events and public relations has always outweighed advertising at first because Mateschitz lacked huge marketing budgets and had to build a reputation for the brand with little cash. Later when Red Bull had plenty of cash for huge marketing budgets, they realised they had created a new marketing model that was far more real and therefore more respected by its customers.

Today Red Bull sells over four billion cans a year in 130 countries with a market share close to 70% worldwide. Mateschitz created an entirely new category of product that many have copied but none have been able to dominate like Red Bull. The brand made Mateschitz a billionaire and the 261st richest person in the world according to *Forbes* magazine. It's said that every Red Bull purchased anywhere in the world puts a quarter of a dollar in Mateschitz's bank account.

Revitalise body and mind
Once the club culture of Europe adopted Red Bull as a staple product to be used for all-night clubbing, retail distributors had little choice but to force a slower selling or less profitable product to the side and replace it with Red Bull.

Moral of the story
A big idea is more valuable than a big advertising budget every time. You've never seen a Google ad, a Skype ad, a Facebook ad, a MySpace ad, a Ben & Jerry's ad, an American Girl ad or an ad for any of hundreds of very successful brands which have never relied on advertising for their success. However, combine a great idea with a great campaign like Red Bull or iPod and you have something more powerful than either on their own.

Smart plan: Part six

You have a product (including the item itself as well as the brand name, packaging and so on), you have a price figured out, you have a distribution plan and now it's time to figure out how you are going to sell your new Smart Battery.

Smart Battery: Exercise six

Step one: Write your creative brief. While doing so you should answer the following questions:

1) What is the specific job of the advertising?
2) Who is our target?
3) What do they currently think (about batteries)?
4) What do we want them to think (about your battery)?
5) What is the single most compelling promise we can make?
6) How do we make it believable?
7) Is there anything else worth considering that may help us get great creative work?

Step two: Where should you advertise it? For a fundamentals book, we're not going to make you develop a media plan with all media costed out. However, you should write a day-in-the-life of your target audience and use that to determine where you should reach your target.

Step three: Develop your Big Idea. Start by writing headlines about for a print ad. Don't write two or three, write at least 50. Let your mind wander to all parts of the battery, how you feel when a battery fails, what it means that this battery lasts ten times as long, why you think this battery is worth more. Explore everything you can think of (for example, safety, environmental impact, convenience, and so on). Once you have your 50 headlines, figure out which three you think are best. Show them to at least five people and see what they think of them. Are they clear? Do they communicate the strategy? If you have a winner, move to the next step; if not, write 50 more headlines.

Step four: Once you have a headline you love and everyone understands, figure out what the big idea is behind the headline. Now, take that idea and figure out how to execute it in every medium you came up with in your day in the life of your target audience. Draw them. Stick figures are fine.

Step five: Test them. Talk to at least five people asking them what they understand the ads to say. Did you communicate what you planned to in your creative brief? If so, well done. If not go back to Step four and do it again.

176   **The Fundamentals of Marketing**

⇐ Distribution channel marketing
➜ **Promotion in marketing**
⇾ Appendix

Assessment

You should have a full marketing plan for the Smart Battery at this time. The only thing left is to develop a plan for how you are going to evaluate the effectiveness of your plan.

1) Determine three financial measures you plan to use to evaluate your effectiveness and rationalise why those are the three best.
2) Determine how you plan to measure your new brand's ongoing health and explain why you chose the particular measures you did.
3) Show how you have proved all the individual elements of your marketing programme will be successful (such as product positioning, pricing, channel marketing strategy, creative strategy, advertising and media selections).
4) Do you think it would be wise to put your plan into test market? Why or why not?

Chapter questions and exercises

1 What brands are you absolutely passionate about? What is it about those brands that make you want to tell friends about them?
2 What brands have you learned about from other friends? What was it about that brand that made them tell you about it?
3 Which do you think is more powerful, a friend's recommendation or a really good ad?
4 What is your favourite ad campaign? Why is it your favourite? How could you make it even better?
5 Describe an ad that you really dislike. What is it about that ad that you dislike so much? How could you make an ad for that same product that was better?
6 Name some big ideas in advertising today.
7 If you could change one thing in the advertising business to make it more ethical, what would that be?

Appendix

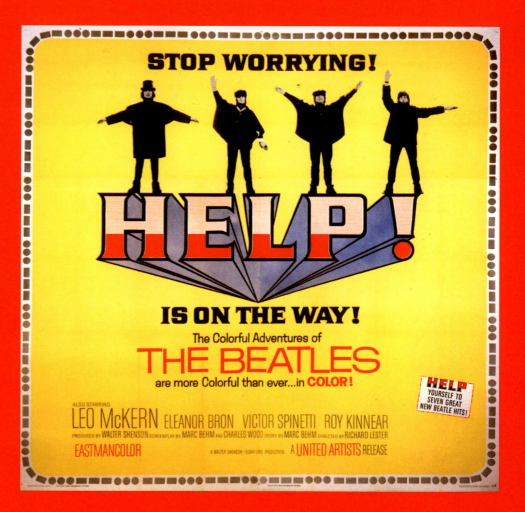

To become a true student of marketing all you have to do is open your eyes. Think about the marketing campaigns that you like. Think about the campaigns that you dislike. Why? Look at brands that are stunningly successful. What made them so successful? Look at brands that are failures. Why did they fail? The questions never end. Seek out advertising, evaluate it and make judgements. You are a consumer. That makes you ultimately qualified to pass judgement.

Take a look at some of the websites listed here to get started on your lifelong learning process.

Student resources

Current news on the marketing and advertising businesses

1) www.adage.com – News, new campaigns, new business from the US.
2) www.adweek.com – News, new campaigns, new business, better regional coverage in the US.
3) www.brandweek.com – Aimed at America's top marketing executives.
4) www.mediaweek.com – Targeting America's top media executives.
5) www.marketingvox.com – Marketing VOX News daily news reported by marketing practitioners covering all marketing topics with an emphasis on online marketing.
6) www.Btobonline.com – Covers the business-to-business online marketing and advertising industry.
7) www.marketingmag.ca – Canadian magazine dedicated to marketing, advertising and media.
8) www.brandrepublic.com – News on marketing in the UK.
9) www.promomagazine.com – Covering all aspects of the sales promotion industry.
10) www.strategymag.com – Magazine for strategic planners in Canada.
11) www.adnews.com.au – Advertising news in Australia.

Information and strategic planning

1) www.demographics.com – American demographic information.
2) www.WARC.com – World Advertising Research Centre. British site with tons of wonderful case study info on it.
3) www.iaaglobal.org – Excellent British site.
4) www.apg.org.uk – A must for up-and-coming account planners.

Creative resources

1) www.luerzersarchive.net – Part of *Luerzer's Archive* magazine. Best archive of advertising that can be accessed by agencies, writers, art directors, etc. This is where you want your work published!
2) www.commarts.com – *Communication Arts* magazine website showing the very best in communications art from around the world.
3) www.boardsmag.com – *Boards* magazine featuring the best in broadcast production from around the world.
4) www.creativehotlist.com – Part of *Communication Arts* magazine. Website shows professional portfolios from around the world.
5) www.agencycompile.com – Good way to see the work of top agencies; also pretty good with new business gossip before it hits the big boys.

Major creative award shows

1) www.canneslions.com – The Cannes Lion is the most prestigious award in the advertising industry.
2) www.dandad.org – Design and art direction, this British site has excellent resources for students in the UK or anywhere.
3) www.clioawards.com – This site has a searchable database that goes back to 1960 in TV, radio, print, poster, design and interactive.
4) www.oneclub.org – Founded 30 years ago, The One Club is the premier association of advertising creatives and students of the industry.
5) www.effie.org – The Effie is the American Marketing Association's award for advertising that produces business results.
6) www.oaaa.org – The Obie is given for excellence in outdoor advertising. In many ways, you'll see the boldest ideas here.
7) www.aaf.org/awards/addy.htm – Part of the American Advertising Federation they give awards on a local and national club level.
8) www.epica-awards.com – This award for advertising creativity started in 1987. The website provides the list of winners for 1996 onwards . They also have the Epica d'Or (overall winner) and the Stone Prize (photography).
9) www.eurobestawards.com – A fairly new award show in Europe.
10) www.webbyawards.com – Website awards.

Professional organisations

1) www.aaf.org – American Advertising Federation. Main educational advertising website with lots of good info for jobseekers.
2) www.aaaa.org – American Association of Advertising Agencies. The main trade organization for the advertising industry in the US. Check out their 'locate an agency' section for finding names and addresses of great agencies in the town of your choice.
3) www.aef.com – Advertising Educational Foundation: some excellent career advice here as well as inspirational characters with great advice.

Job seeking

1) www.talentzoo.com – Becoming a pretty good job-posting site just for advertising.
2) www.jobbound.com – The best source of information about preparing to get a job in the advertising business.
3) www.adage.com, www.adweek.com, www.monster.com, www.careerbuilder.com, etc.

Industry rumours and gossip

1) www.adrants.com – Often irreverent, always informative.
2) www.Ihaveanidea.com – Great blog with lots of interviews with prominent ad people.
3) www.adholes.com – As they say – Ad Industry Schmoozing without expensive restaurant tabs.
4) www.albinoblacksheep.com/flash/yatta.php – Just silly, but it can be fun!
5) www.adverblog.com – Global advertising blog with 100+ topics.

There are hundreds of sites dedicated to advertising and marketing around the world. Decide your own favourites and view them often as they are ever-changing.

Must-read books

1) *Confessions of an Advertising Man*: David Ogilvy's classic from 1963 holds up remarkably well all these years later.
2) *Disruption*: Jean Marie Dru. The first half of this book is amazing and may be the best advertising book ever written. The second half and sequel I found a bit tedious.
3) *The Do it Yourself Lobotomy* by Tom Monahan – a terrific book on creative development.
4) *Positioning*: Trout & Ries – a business classic.
5) *What Sticks*: Briggs & Stuart study what advertising actually works in the marketplace.
6) *Hey Whipple, Squeeze This* by Luke Sullivan – a funny look at creating great advertising ideas.
7) *Up the Agency* by Peter Mayle. From the author of *A Year in Provence*, a funny look into the advertising business he started in.
8) *20 Ads the Shook the World*: Twitchell. A look at 20 iconic campaigns and where they came from.
9) *Where the Suckers Moon*: Rothenburg. A must-read for anyone in new business.
10) *Hoopla*: the inside story of Crispin Porter + Bogusky, one of the most award-winning agencies in the world.
11) *Creative Advertising*: Mario Pricken's book on creating great campaigns.
12) *Truth Lies and Advertising*: Jon Steel's book on account planning.
13) *The Tipping Point*: Gladwell's demonstration of how ideas become trends and change the world.

That should keep you busy for a while….

Glossary of terminology

Advertiser: The manufacturer, retailer, or supplier that advertises their products and services.

Advertising: Traditionally, paid communication on behalf of a marketer designed to persuade consumers into taking action. According to consumers, any communication on behalf of a brand is advertising.

Advertising budget: Money budgeted to be spent on the promotion of a brand.

Advertising research: Research conducted to determine and improve the effectiveness of advertising.

Agency commission: A method of paying an advertising agency that allots a percentage of the cost of the media buy to the agency.

Billings: Total amount a client pays for the purchase of media time or space.

Brand: Name, sign or symbol used to distinguish one manufacturer's product or service from another.

Brand development index (BDI): A comparison of the percentage of a brand's sales in a market to the percentage of the national population in that same market used to determine strong and weak markets for a particular brand.

Brand manager: Person responsible for marketing a specific brand.

Category development index (CDI): A comparison of the percentage of sales of a product category in a market, to the percentage of population in that market used to determine strong and weak markets for a particular product category.

Channels of distribution: The route a product goes through from manufacturer to consumers including wholesalers, retailers, etc.

Client: An advertising agency's term for the advertisers it serves.

Consumer behaviour: Study of how people obtain and use products (and services).

Copy: The text of an advert.

Cost per thousand (CPM): The cost, per 1000 people reached.

Creative boutique: An agency that focuses only on providing creative (ads) to its clients and does not provide media planning, research, etc.

Creatives: The art directors, copywriters and production personnel in an advertising agency.

Creative strategy: A document telling a creative team made up of an art director and copywriter what message should be conveyed and to whom in order to sell the product or service. How that message is told is referred to as the 'execution'.

Demographics: Basic descriptive classifications of consumers, such as age, sex, income, education, size of household, ownership of home, etc.

Direct marketing: Sending your message directly to consumers. Includes Direct mail, Telemarketing and Internet.

Focus group: Research method that brings together a small group of consumers to discuss the product or advertising, under the direction of a moderator.

Frequency: Number of times a person sees your ad within a given time period (usually four weeks).

Full-service agency: An agency that handles all aspects of the advertising process, including planning, design, production, placement, public relations, sales promotion, and direct marketing.

Gross rating points (GRPs): A measure of the advertising weight calculated by multiplying the ads reach times the four- week frequency.

Integrated marketing communication (IMC): A buzzword of the 1990s, IMC is the organisation of all forms of a brand's communications around a central brand idea.

Marketer: A business that develops, manufacturers and markets goods and services to the consumer.

Marketing: The manipulation of product features, pricing, packaging, advertising, merchandising, distribution, and marketing budget to maximise sales and/or profitability.

Market share: The percentage of a product category sales, in terms of dollars or units.

Media plan: A plan designed to maximise the impact of the advertising on the chosen target audience.

Medium (plural, media): A way of transferring information, news, entertainment, and advertising messages to an audience such as television, magazines, radio, Internet, billboards, etc.

Parity products: Products from different manufacturers that have functionally equivalent attributes, for example aspirin is a parity product regardless of the number of brands of aspirin on the market.

Pre-testing: Testing a strategy or advertisement prior to placing the ad in the media.

Private label brand: Brand owned by a retailer.

Product differentiation: How your product is different from your competition.

Product life cycle: A marketing theory where brands follow a set pattern of introduction, growth, maturity, and then sales decline.

Product positioning: How a consumer perceives a brand compared to its competition.

Promotion: One of the 4 'P's' of marketing that includes all forms of communication on a brand's behalf. Commonly used when talking about sales promotion that includes discounts, retailer allowances, premium offers, coupons, contests, sweepstakes, etc.

Psychographics: Terms that describe consumers on the basis of psychological characteristics.

Qualitative research: Small-scale research that emphasises the quality of consumer perceptions and attitudes; for example, in-depth interviews and focus groups.

Quantitative research: Large-scale projectable research that emphasising consumer trends.

Reach: Percentage of individuals reached at least once during a specific period of time (usually four weeks).

Sales promotion: Marketing activities such as couponing, sweepstakes and so on designed to stimulate immediate sales.

Scanner: An optical device that reads UPC label (universal pricing code). Used at check-out in most stores, this machine helps retailers not only keep track of pricing, but inventory management.

Seasonality: A variation in sales quantities throughout the year.

Segmentation: Dividing consumers into groups based on selected demographics or psychographics so that each can be marketed to in the most appropriate way possible.

Situation analysis: The evaluation of information about a brand's marketing efforts and also of their competition's to assess the overall marketing environment.

Strategic planning: Determination of 'what' you should do in order to grow your brand.

Tag line: A line at the end of an advertisement that sums up the brand/campaign like (such as Nike's Just do it).

Target audience: A certain demographic group you want to reach.

Target market: A group an advertiser believes is most likely to purchase their product or service and therefore is the main group of people the advertiser wishes to aim their advertising messages toward.

Picture credits and acknowledgements

Picture credits

Acknowledgements

Thanks to all my amazingly supportive colleagues at Syracuse University's S.I. Newhouse School of Public Communications for giving me the opportunity to teach at one of the best communications schools in the entire world. Special thanks to Professor Emiritus John Philip Jones for introducing me to the good people at AVA Publishing, for your inspiring 13+ books and counting and for your decades of brilliant teaching and practice. You are a legend and an inspiration to us all.

Thanks to my many inspiring bosses throughout my career who challenged me to do more and be more than I ever thought I would. Mike, Reiner and Mary, you're the very best this business ever had. Thank you!

Thanks to Georgia Kennedy, Ann Middlebrook and Brian Morris of AVA Publishing for their patience with a new author, your encouragement, direction and for allowing more than one deadline to become elastic.

Thanks to my family for your understanding support as I wrote this book – twice! Rebecca, I promise we'll hike the Northville-Placid trail, Emily thanks for saying I'd never finish this book (look, it's done!) and Kirsten, let's go see Maine or anything else you'd like to see in this spectacular world.

And to my students… thanks to each and every one of you! I've learned more from you than I've taught. I sincerely hope you live dreams bigger than you ever imagined.

All the very best.

Lynne Elvins/Naomi Goulder

Working with ethics

The Fundamentals of Marketing

Publisher's note

The subject of ethics is not new, yet its consideration within the applied visual arts is perhaps not as prevalent as it might be. Our aim here is to help a new generation of students, educators and practitioners find a methodology for structuring their thoughts and reflections in this vital area.

AVA Publishing hopes that these **Working with ethics** pages provide a platform for consideration and a flexible method for incorporating ethical concerns in the work of educators, students and professionals. Our approach consists of four parts:

The **introduction** is intended to be an accessible snapshot of the ethical landscape, both in terms of historical development and current dominant themes.

The **framework** positions ethical consideration into four areas and poses questions about the practical implications that might occur. Marking your response to each of these questions on the scale shown will allow your reactions to be further explored by comparison.

The **case study** sets out a real project and then poses some ethical questions for further consideration. This is a focus point for a debate rather than a critical analysis so there are no predetermined right or wrong answers.

A selection of **further reading** for you to consider areas of particular interest in more detail.

Introduction

Ethics is a complex subject that interlaces the idea of responsibilities to society with a wide range of considerations relevant to the character and happiness of the individual. It concerns virtues of compassion, loyalty and strength, but also of confidence, imagination, humour and optimism. As introduced in ancient Greek philosophy, the fundamental ethical question is *what should I do?* How we might pursue a 'good' life not only raises moral concerns about the effects of our actions on others, but also personal concerns about our own integrity.

In modern times the most important and controversial questions in ethics have been the moral ones. With growing populations and improvements in mobility and communications, it is not surprising that considerations about how to structure our lives together on the planet should come to the forefront. For visual artists and communicators it should be no surprise that these considerations will enter into the creative process.

Some ethical considerations are already enshrined in government laws and regulations or in professional codes of conduct. For example, plagiarism and breaches of confidentiality can be punishable offences. Legislation in various nations makes it unlawful to exclude people with disabilities from accessing information or spaces. The trade of ivory as a material has been banned in many countries. In these cases, a clear line has been drawn under what is unacceptable. But most ethical matters remain open to debate, among experts and lay-people alike, and in the end we have to make our own choices on the basis of our own guiding principles or values. Is it more ethical to work for a charity than for a commercial company? Is it unethical to create something that others find ugly or offensive?

Specific questions such as these may lead to other questions that are more abstract. For example, is it only effects on humans (and what they care about) that are important, or might effects on the natural world require attention too? Is promoting ethical consequences justified even when it requires ethical sacrifices along the way? Must there be a single unifying theory of ethics (such as the Utilitarian thesis that the right course of action is always the one that leads to the greatest happiness of the greatest number), or might there always be many different ethical values that pull a person in various directions?

As we enter into ethical debate and engage with these dilemmas on a personal and professional level, we may change our views or change our view of others. The real test though is whether, as we reflect on these matters, we change the way we act as well as the way we think. Socrates, the 'father' of philosophy, proposed that people will naturally do 'good' if they know what is right. But this point might only lead us to yet another question: *how do we know what is right?*

You
What are your ethical beliefs?

Central to everything you do will be your attitude to people and issues around you. For some people their ethics are an active part of the decisions they make everyday as a consumer, a voter or a working professional. Others may think about ethics very little and yet this does not automatically make them unethical. Personal beliefs, lifestyle, politics, nationality, religion, gender, class or education can all influence your ethical viewpoint.

Using the scale, where would you place yourself? What do you take into account to make your decision? Compare results with your friends or colleagues.

Your client
What are your terms?

Working relationships are central to whether ethics can be embedded into a project and your conduct on a day-to-day basis is a demonstration of your professional ethics. The decision with the biggest impact is whom you choose to work with in the first place. Cigarette companies or arms traders are often-cited examples when talking about where a line might be drawn, but rarely are real situations so extreme. At what point might you turn down a project on ethical grounds and how much does the reality of having to earn a living effect your ability to choose?

Using the scale, where would you place a project? How does this compare to your personal ethical level?

01 02 03 04 05 06 07 08 09 10

01 02 03 04 05 06 07 08 09 10

Your specifications
What are the impacts of your materials?

In relatively recent times we are learning that many natural materials are in short supply. At the same time we are increasingly aware that some man-made materials can have harmful, long-term effects on people or the planet. How much do you know about the materials that you use? Do you know where they come from, how far they travel and under what conditions they are obtained? When your creation is no longer needed, will it be easy and safe to recycle? Will it disappear without a trace? Are these considerations the responsibility of you or are they out of your hands?

Using the scale, mark how ethical your material choices are.

Your creation
What is the purpose of your work?

Between you, your colleagues and an agreed brief, what will your creation achieve? What purpose will it have in society and will it make a positive contribution? Should your work result in more than commercial success or industry awards? Might your creation help save lives, educate, protect or inspire? Form and function are two established aspects of judging a creation, but there is little consensus on the obligations of visual artists and communicators toward society, or the role they might have in solving social or environmental problems. If you want recognition for being the creator, how responsible are you for what you create and where might that responsibility end?

Using the scale, mark how ethical the purpose of your work is.

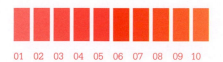

01 02 03 04 05 06 07 08 09 10

01 02 03 04 05 06 07 08 09 10

One aspect of marketing that raises an ethical dilemma is the extent to which marketing techniques might persuade or influence consumers to purchase items that they may not need or that may even be detrimental. Central to this question is the balance of power in the relationship between the seller and the buyer. Marketers emphasise the positive attributes of a product or service and cement favourable associations in the minds of the target audience, usually to generate sales. In free markets, buyers should be able to compare and choose from a variety of competitive options. However, as marketing has become increasingly diverse in its formats and complex in its application of psychological techniques, questions can be raised about the freedom of individuals to choose fairly. Do marketers genuinely feel positive about the products and services that they help to promote, or are they driven purely to make profit for themselves and the seller? Should marketing people have responsibility for ensuring that buyers can make fully informed choices? Or is this issue already taken care of through independent consumer groups and anti-trust law?

In the mid-1980s, the social marketing of condoms emerged as an effective tool in the fight to combat the spread of HIV/AIDS. Programmes made condoms available, affordable and acceptable in countries affected by the epidemic, particularly in sub-Saharan Africa, and used marketing messages to raise awareness of the disease.

Complex cultural factors can present a challenge for HIV prevention, education and condom promotion. For example, due to gender inequalities, young girls and women are regularly and repeatedly denied information about, and access to, condoms. Therefore, condoms must be marketed in ways that help to overcome sexual and personal obstacles to their use.

One marketing technique that might be deployed is to recruit prominent individuals and groups to deliver and endorse safer sex messages. This approach has been successful through the recruitment of sports and music figures, religious leaders and politicians. In 1996, Archbishop Tutu delivered an impassioned plea for South Africans to face the facts about HIV and AIDS in a television documentary entitled The Rubber Revolution. Tutu, along with Catholic and Muslim leaders and various national sports figures, discussed the importance of open conversations about sexuality and HIV/AIDS. Prior to Tutu's involvement, the South African Broadcasting Corporation had not allowed the word 'condom' to be used on primetime television.

The Society for Family Health (SFH) in Nigeria also launched a high-profile marketing campaign using former world-class football star, Sunday Oliseh, who is a prominent role model in Nigeria. SFH produced print, radio and television messages with Oliseh promoting Gold Circle, a specially created brand of condom, along with condom use and the practice of safer sex. The campaign was launched simultaneously with the 1998 World Cup Soccer tournament, in which Oliseh led the national team.

With support from USAID and other non-profit organisations, the condom brand Prudence was introduced to Zaire in 1996. Previous to this campaign, the total number of condoms given away or sold in Zaire was approximately 500,000 a year. In 1999, four million Prudence condoms were sold. A key tactic in the marketing campaign was the placement and pricing strategy. By selling Prudence condoms via street hawkers at three cents each, people were able to get hold of condoms anywhere at any time. Salespeople were also supported with Prudence key rings, bartender aprons, calendars, hats and signs; and music events offered half-price admission to anyone with a Prudence pack. The marketing campaign has been so successful that Zairians now use 'Prudence' as a generic term for a condom.

Is it more ethical to practice social marketing than purely commercial marketing?

Is it unethical to pay somebody to endorse a product or service that they may not otherwise use?

Would you work on a project to market condoms in African countries?

There is an increasing political and social consensus that something needs to be done to safeguard children from the worst excesses of direct marketing and the pressures of commercialisation.

Reverend Dr Rowan Williams,
the Archbishop of Canterbury

AIGA
Design business and ethics
2007, AIGA

Eaton, Marcia Muelder
Aesthetics and the good life
1989, Associated University Press

Ellison, David
Ethics and aesthetics in European modernist literature
2001, Cambridge University Press

Fenner, David EW (Ed.)
Ethics and the arts: an anthology
1995, Garland Reference Library of Social Science

Gini, Al (Ed.)
Case studies in business ethics
2005, Prentice Hall

McDonough, William and Braungart, Michael
'Cradle to Cradle: Remaking the Way We Make Things'
2002

Papanek, Victor
'Design for the Real World: Making to Measure'
1971

United Nations
Global Compact the Ten Principles www.unglobalcompact.org/AboutTheGC/
TheTenPrinciples/index.html